COMMON SENSE

Joseph McSorley

OF THE PAULIST FATHERS

COMMON SENSE

THE BRUCE PUBLISHING COMPANY
MILWAUKEE

IMPRIMI POTEST
  EUGENE M. BURKE, C.S.P.

CUM PERMISSU SUPERIORUM
  WM. A. MICHELL, C.S.P.
  Superior General

NIHIL OBSTAT
  JOHN A. SCHULIEN, S.T.D.
  Censor librorum

IMPRIMATUR
  ✠ALBERTUS G. MEYER
  Archiepiscopus Milwauchiensis

  Die 17ª Junii, 1957

Library of Congress Catalog Card Number: 57–12563

FOR THEIR INDISPENSABLE AID
IN ITS MAKING
THIS BOOK
IS GRATEFULLY DEDICATED
TO
GERTRUDE A. TRAGESER
HELEN MEYER
ANN F. COLLIGAN

"SEEK FOR TRUTH AMIDST THE ERROR, ESTABLISH ITS EXISTENCE, APPLAUD IT, AND ENDEAVOR TO MAKE IT A BASIS FOR FURTHER TRUTH AND A FULCRUM FOR THE OVERTHROW OF THE ERROR CONNECTED WITH IT."   —*Father Hecker*

CONTENTS

CONTENTS

III

COMMON SENSE

THE "COMMON SENSE"

Despite the jest about common sense being extremely uncommon, we all recognize the high value of opinions that are shared by most men. Minted into proverbs or axioms and widely distributed, the common sense helps to keep truth from being overlooked or distorted; it often forestalls unwise decisions and prevents foolish actions. As might be anticipated in view of her universal mission, the Church has high respect for the general opinion of men. In her schools we are trained to lean heavily on views held "always, everywhere, and by everybody." We are taught that "the world's judgment is a safe judgment." To be sure, it would be fanciful to imagine that — apart from divine revelation, divinely preserved — we ever come upon opinions literally universal; but we do find views which are widespread and enduring; and these are helpful guides to truth. The Church's respect for them reminds us of the theory that memories of the primitive revelation were spread widely through the world as the race scattered into different areas; and that these traditions were handed down from generation to generation, framed in the thought forms and the languages of many different peoples. Thus ancient wisdom, plus experience, helped to create proverbs which embodied and preserved common sense.

In the measure that the old habit of reverence fades away, venerable sayings with their embodiment of "common sense" have to yield place to upstart cynical substitutes which flatly contradict tradition. Half seriously, we may be advised, "Let the youngest speak first and oftenest"; "Never do today what can be put off till tomorrow." Yet, this attempted revolution cannot quite drive time-tested axioms from men's minds any more than the ancient burning of the libraries of Alexandria or the modern destruction of the intellectual treasures of Louvain could dam up the ceaseless flow of learning. Sayings reflecting "common sense" will survive the generations that ignore or attempt to destroy them. Views that have sunk their roots into the general mind still command attention; even a pygmy, if mounted on the shoulders of a giant, can still look over the head of a very tall man. "Truth is mighty and will prevail." Progress is always compatible with "a decent respect to the opinions of mankind." Alexander Pope gave this good advice:

> Be not the first by whom the new are tried,
> Nor yet the last to lay the old aside.

Quite in harmony with decent regard for common sense is the phrase coined in early Christian ages by the great Tertullian, who built his argument for the faith on the premise that "The human soul is naturally Christian." In other words, he held that man is naturally disposed to accept the Gospel. Down through the centuries, recognition of this principle led missionaries to imitate the technique used by St. Paul in his sermon before the Areopagus. They based the truth they were about to present upon convictions already held by their hearers.

As above noted, "common sense" is often conveyed in the form of proverbs and axioms, reflecting the experience of the common man who passes on to his neighbors what he himself has learned the hard way. The history of proverbs in the English-speaking world is especially interesting. They attained an extraordinary degree of popularity in the Elizabethan age and thereafter declined — although those coined by Shakespeare possessed and have retained a sort of unique authority. These facts, placed before us by experts in the history of English literature, seem to imply that the traditional method of publicizing the "common sense" of England fell into disuse about the same time that the religious unity of England collapsed. There is the further rather significant coincidence that Shakespeare, who was the chief surviving author of popular proverbs, echoed the teaching of the Church so consistently that many regarded this habit as evidence of his own personal Catholicity. Shakespeare believed that mercy "blesseth him that gives and him that takes." As for ambition, he tells us "by that sin fell the angels." We learn that "the blackest sin is cleared with absolution." And the dying Henry VI asks God to forgive him and to forgive his murderer as well: "Oh God forgive my sins, and pardon thee." An able critic writes that Shakespeare's men and women "are the mouthpieces of thoughts tinged with the proverbs that are as surely a part of their background as they were of their creator's."

After Shakespeare's rich contribution, we depend chiefly on poetic phrases so quickly adopted and so long retained that they deserve to be classed with proverbs as indicative of the "common sense." Conspicuous among the poets to whom we are indebted in this respect, have been Wordsworth, Browning, Tennyson, and also, of course, Faber and Francis Thompson. Men still cherish such lines as: "The world is too much with us." "A man's reach must exceed his grasp." "More things are done by prayer than this world dreams of." "Closer is He than breathing, and nearer than hands and feet." "All things betray thee, who betrayest Me." Nor should we forget the height to which Kipling rose when, through his "Recessional," the England which had once been "Mary's dower" seemed to find its soul again and speak aloud of the infinity of God, the worth of prayer, the matchless dignity of "a humble and a contrite heart."

The topic of "common sense" must not be abandoned without recalling that modern defenders of the Catholic faith have been well aware of the advantage of building upon ideals and convictions endorsed by the common sense of those persons to whom the faith was being recommended. Newman's approach along this line is fairly obvious throughout his writings. Father Hecker also, in two books that made history in their day — *Questions of the Soul* and *Aspirations of Nature* — undertook to show the spiritually earnest men of his own generation that the solution of their problems and the fulfilling of their aspirations could be found with the aid of the Catholic Church. The first volume stressed the nature of man's destiny, the validity of his longing for the perfect life, and the role of asceticism in attaining union with God. The second volume was directed specifically to those non-Catholic Americans who were supporting social principles that contradicted their own professed religious beliefs, but harmonized well with the teachings of the Church.

What has been written in the present brief discussion of a most important theme should at least help to show how practical it might be to collect proverbs and quotations, favored by a large multitude of persons over a long period of time, all of which display deep sympathy with, and often definite belief in, principles and teachings characteristic of Catholicism. A book written along these lines would be a demonstration that numerous Catholic ideals and Catholic teachings are at least equivalently endorsed by "common sense." Surely it would not be hard to prove that our fellow citizens realize the indispensable necessity of authority in all activities involving the vital interests of the whole population — in a panic for instance, or during an earthquake, an epidemic, a war. They understand that personal morality is based on something more than mere personal expediency. And they recognize that a man does a noble deed when, at the cost of his own life, he saves other persons from agonizing death.

One more phenomenon of our times that seems worthy of notice is the wide response of the outside world to the mystical ideals presented by the Church. Within the memory of living man, many illustrations of this have been presented: for example, the manifestation of deep interest in the revelations of Mother Juliana; the steadily growing use of the "teachings" of the barefooted lay Carmelite, Brother Lawrence; the selections which have appeared in the Clarendon Press collection of English mystical verse. The scholarly editors of this Oxford publication, noting that mysticism "has emerged from the morass of apathy which characterized the eighteenth and the greater part of the nineteenth century . . . conclude that the world is undergoing a spiritual revitalization." And they give large space to writers who present Catholic ideals and Catholic teachings. They have done this in their effort "to show that the torch of the Inner Life has been handed down from age to age until the present day."

I.

"THE UNKNOWN GOD"

WHEN St. Paul, on one of his mission journeys, entered the city of Athens, he found an altar dedicated "To the Unknown God." A little later, in the first Christian sermon preached to the Gentiles, he made a reference to it. "And it is this unknown object of your devotion that I am revealing to you. The God who made the world and all that is in it . . . does not dwell in temples that our hands have made. . . ." "He, who gives to all of us life and breath and all we have . . . He is not far from anyone of us; it is in Him that we live, and move, and have our being; thus, some of your own poets have told us. For indeed, we are His children."

We can learn much from considering a child's approach to God. If well instructed, the child usually possesses a fairly good notion of God, believing what he has been told: that God is good and kind and loving; that He is present everywhere; that we are completely dependent upon Him; that we should be careful never to displease Him. As the child grows older, certain puzzling questions present themselves: "Who made God?"; "If He is here, why do we not see Him?"; "If He can do everything, why does He let people get sick?"; "If He made everything, who made bad things like poison and snakes?"

Whoever undertakes to answer questions that occur to a

8

child's mind, should be careful to give replies that are true so far as they go — replies that make sense, even if not perfectly satisfying. Otherwise, a basis is laid for future trouble. As the young person grows older and encounters problems more and more puzzling, for these, also, he should receive a true — if only partial — explanation. It is by this sort of procedure that each of us must grow in wisdom. Content for the moment with answers that give no more than temporary satisfaction, men go on gradually to fuller knowledge. Physicists, astronomers, philosophers make progress slowly, as they deal patiently with problems of ever increasing complexity. Partial answers open the way to further knowledge. It is the same in the field of religion.

For centuries the Church, following St. Paul, has been engaged in correcting imperfect notions of God. She has condemned numerous heresies, some of them subtle, some of them gross, some of them absurd. In her teaching, she draws upon divinely given sources — Holy Scripture and apostolic tradition; and when she presents revealed truths to the faithful, she defines them in the precise language of theology. Her definitions, although infallibly true, cannot exhaust the content of the truths defined, which deal with what is supernatural, infinite, divine, and therefore literally "incomprehensible"; for the human intellect cannot *comprehend* — that is to say, exhaust — the content of such terms as "eternity," "omniscience," "the Blessed Trinity." But working within the protective barriers of the definitions, scholars and saints — busy as scientific research workers — deepen and enrich man's knowledge of God.

Holy persons, and particularly mystical saints, who plunge into the depths of unfathomable truth, discover new implications and applications of what is already known; at times they come into contact with what they find themselves unable even to describe. Thus St. Paul speaks of his own experiences as something quite beyond human power to put into words. St. John of the Cross, St. Teresa, and others, referring to what they have learned in prayer, repeat, almost like a refrain, such words as "dark," "obscure," "hidden," "secret," "cloud," "mystical."

Telling the story of their own approach to God, translating old truths into new words and modern language, saints have enlightened generation after generation, and have distributed the bread of heaven to multitudes. When we study the path they followed, we perceive that they made progress not so much by way of imagination and intellect, as by willing, aspiring, renouncing. They practiced that purest form of loving which is possible only to a soul purged of egotism — the soul that surrenders to God unreservedly. And this must be the first and foremost of our desires — the longing to give ourselves completely to God, unseen, incomprehensible, infinite, but always present, always loving. Thus, to use St. Paul's words, we may hope eventually to see Him no longer through a glass darkly, but face to face, to know Him as we are known.

THE TRINITY

EARLY in our approach to the idea of God, we face the doctrine that God is a Trinity. As a careful reading of the New Testament shows, this mysterious truth was part of Christ's revelation to His disciples. The doctrine plainly involves no contradiction; it does not assert that one God is three Gods, or that three Persons are one Person. Nevertheless, it does remain a mystery, a truth of faith based on revelation; it is not demonstrable, not totally comprehensible. St. Patrick, when instructing pagans, made his famous comparison by holding up a three-leaved shamrock. This, however, is an illustration only; and the Church, deeply concerned to keep the divine Unity from being obscured, has been obliged to censure many well-meaning attempts to frame a theological formulation of the doctrine of the Trinity. Indeed, centuries passed before a satisfying definition was officially adopted.

As finally formulated, the Catholic doctrine includes these truths:

1. There is, and there can be, only one God.

2. The distinction into Father, Son, and Holy Spirit affects what theologians call God's *inner* life.

3. Every divine activity in the created universe implies the participation of all three divine Persons as a single principle. In other words, we have been created by God — Father, Son, and Holy Spirit; we strive to live in obedience to, and in com-

munion with, Father, Son, and Holy Spirit; when we adore
God, the one complete object of our worship is the undivided
Trinity.

Although every divine activity in creation really involves
all three Persons, we sometimes — by using a theological figure
of speech — ascribe one activity to one Person, another activity
to another Person. That is to say, we *appropriate* a particular
divine activity in the created world to one of the three Persons,
because of the similarity of this activity to the personal characteristic of Father, or Son, or Holy Spirit, as the case may be.
Thus we may speak of creation as the work of the Father;
of sanctification as the work of the Holy Spirit. But we understand — at least, we should understand — that in each of these
activities all three Persons are co-operating.

An outstanding example of "appropriation" is presented in
the Church's teaching on the indwelling of the Holy Ghost.
The liturgy bids us pray, "Come Holy Ghost"; it speaks of the
Holy Ghost "coming to dwell in the soul." These expressions
suggest a consideration of what is meant by God's indwelling.

GOD'S PRESENCE

THE child who enters upon his mental life with calm confidence that things are what they seem to be, will, after a few years, begin to question and argue about the reality that underlies appearance. Fortunate is he if, in the early phases of intellectual development, he is guided by persons willing and able to impart some of the lessons they learned while facing and solving problems for themselves. One of the Church's chief cares has ever been to assist competent teachers of religion in the task of formulating abstract, or puzzling, spiritual truths in terms intelligible to the average man of good will. In connection with this she pays careful attention to the task of making plain the correct meaning of each word used in a doctrinal statement.

Here, for example, are one or two fundamental ideas which must be understood by anyone who desires to know what he should believe about God:

First, as to "Being." Being is that which exists. Obviously, the First Being cannot have received existence from another being. In other words, the First Being could have no cause of existence outside Itself; nor could it have been limited, or confined, by anything outside Itself. The First Being must have been everlasting, necessary, infinite. It created other beings by giving them secondary, or contingent, existence.

Among the many errors that spring from false concepts about

13

God, these two are conspicuous: (1) that God is active in this world only, not outside of it; (2) that God is active outside the world, but not within it. Both notions are plainly irreconcilable with belief in God's infinity. He lives and is active both in this world and outside it; He is immanent; He is transcendent. We cannot get even a good "working notion" of the Infinite One, unless we reject the theory that confines God to the universe, and the countertheory which excludes Him from it. We have to realize that He is here, there, everywhere, in each nook, and corner; "closer to us than breathing"; and at the same time He is "out beyond the shining of the farthest star."

When we say that God is present in a particular place, we do not mean that He is "present" in the same sense that water is present in a bowl, or a chair present in a room. We get nearer to the true idea, if we think of heat, light, gravitation, magnetism, electricity, which are real and present, although they remain imperceptible to the senses until they are made known to us through their effects. Even though unable to draw a picture, or make a true mental image of them, we do manage to learn a great deal about them, and to reach some very important conclusions about their characteristics. Remembering this, we begin to see what is meant by the statement that a spirit is present where it is active, and as it is active.

God, present in the universe, keeps it existing; if He ceased to be present, it would no longer exist. He is present in the *whole* universe; for He gave all things existence and keeps them existing. He is present in the human soul; in one way as the Giver of life; in another way as the Giver of intelligence and will; and, in still another way, as the Giver of divine grace.

We say quite truly that God is no less present to us than we are present to ourselves. He brought us into being; He keeps us existing; He knows us through and through; He is perfectly

aware of our thoughts, desires, temptations, failures. It is out-
rageous for me to disobey God who is dwelling within my
soul, and to offend Him will necessarily involve some sort of
punishment; yet, on the other hand, He is ever ready to forgive offenses, and to reward good deeds most generously. Like
a ceaseless pulsation of energy within, God's activity strengthens
the soul against the urges of temptation, making it a fit and
ready instrument for the doing of His will. If we develop the
habit of being sensitively aware of this at all times and in all
places, we shall move steadily toward our goal — immeasurable,
perfect peace and everlasting joy.

ORDER

ORDER reflects the mind of God. It is, therefore, heaven's first law. But that statement requires some clarification.

If a man were to say, "I always begin at the end," shallow thinkers might imagine he was out of order. But he would actually be affirming a principle fundamental in all intelligent activity. For one must first choose an end, and then decide on the means to achieve it; it is in relation to the end in view that a pattern is classified as orderly, or otherwise. Apparent disorder which serves a purpose not yet obvious to the observer, may nevertheless be really good order. When we decipher a code, break down a confused financial statement, solve a problem in chemistry, physics, biology, or engineering by a series of experiments, we are arriving at order hidden under superficial disorder. Wise men do this sometimes in interpreting the actions of their fellow men, sometimes in trying to discover the will of God, hidden under what seems incompatible with God's love and providence. Readiness to wait patiently until an explanation is found — no matter how long it may be deferred — is characteristic of faith. So, when facing seemingly purposeless, cruel events, the saint goes instantly to the solution by accepting those events as part of the inexplicable, invisible, "permissive" will of God. Whenever we confront reality, whether in the mind of men; in the material, or the spiritual

world; in the infinitesimal particles of matter; or in the farthest
limits of space; there always we meet with laws, with order.

Any lasting achievement, any intelligent attempt to discover
or invent something new, is related to an explicit or implicit
belief in the reign of law. This was never so obviously true as
now, when research in every imaginable field is presenting
us with fruits that follow the discovering of nature's order. In
comparatively recent years men have found out that certain
laws hold each atom together; that they keep countless satellites
— including our earth — revolving around central suns; that
they fix the place of the constellations and control the direction
and the rate of their movement. "Nuclear fission," "antibiotics,"
"polio vaccine," "psychosomatic medicine" are new words which
reflect the practical importance of recent discoveries. Current
medical science stresses the tendency of a disordered body to
disturb the order of the mind, and vice versa; and the word
"psychosomatic" reminds us not only of the reign of law in
human life, but also and most importantly of the constant
interaction that goes on between the physical and the mental
spheres. Attention to this universal, orderly activity is a primary
dictate of reason. Countless concentric circles may revolve
smoothly; but if we shift the center of even one, there is
confusion; all is disturbed, until each particular realm or level
is again in proper relationship with the higher.

When activity on a lower level is not subordinated to activity
on the higher, the lower superficial "order" becomes disorder;
and disorder is a caricature of reality. Spiritually speaking, an
infringement of order either on the lower or the higher level
may involve danger of disease, insanity, death. As the physical
ranks below the spiritual, so must the natural rank below the
supernatural. If we conceived of the universe as a circle, of
which God is the center, then, we might say that the average
man seems to be trying to turn it into an ellipse, a sort of

distorted circle which, instead of one center, has two focal points, himself and God. The absurd attempt is motivated by foolish egotism, absurd self-exaggeration. Who except the saints actually centers every thought and word and deed and wish and plan on God? Yet the fixed point with which every thought and word and deed must be concentric is necessarily the center established by the divine will.

The medieval recluse, Juliana of Norwich, saw God as a point: "I saw God in a Point," wrote Juliana, "the mid Point at the center of all things." That is to say, all light, all energy, all law was radiating out from God, the Mid-Point of the universe, to the farthest limits of creation. In our scale of values, it is always the standard established by God's will which makes a thing precious or worthless. Unless we adjust ourselves to that pattern we involve ourselves in an imaginary order, a pseudo order, a *disorder* which leads inevitably to chaos.

On the supernatural level, disorder implies an approach to sin. To anything disorderly, theologians apply the term "inordinate"; that is to say, they declare it "automatically wrong." Hence each of us may find it wise to check ourselves occasionally by measuring our words, our actions, and even our thoughts and desires, according to God's unchangeable standard. We must try to make sure that nothing for which we are responsible can be classified as too high or too low, too big or too little, too fast or too slow, too hard or too soft, too gentle or too stern, too early or too late! We must be neither too strong nor too weak, too introverted nor too extroverted. The standard for everything is set by that ancient phrase, so conspicuous in Catholic tradition, *Nequid nimis* — "Nothing in excess."

God's aim in creating a free creature is to obtain wholehearted obedience and love from a being who is able to refuse. Man's ideal relationship with the Creator is, of course, absolute dependence; obviously therefore, his only proper attitude is

adoration. Free service should be his glad offering. Aware of
dependence, the creature should adore; and adoration, if practiced steadily, will bring growth in holiness and ultimately
Godlikeness and perfect union.

Actually, man is able to rebel, to turn away. Such base
ingratitude is madness; and in theory it seems unlikely that an
intelligent being would commit spiritual suicide by consciously
violating the order established by his Creator. But experience
corrects this mistaken anticipation; and indeed, each one of us
at times does try to get something despite God's disapproval.
Obviously these attempts cannot ever bring us anything worth
retaining, or possible to retain. And there is the further serious
consequence that disobedience will forfeit gifts which would
be ours were we to conform to the will of God, so far as we
are able to ascertain it. Yet we continue to fall short.

Looking for a "rule of thumb" to guide us in our activities,
we may begin as the saints begin. With them, God's will is
always the central interest; and to that center their whole order
of life is adjusted. We too, in humble fashion, may make
God's will our rule of life, trying to make sure that in our
planning and our doing, we put first the things which are
first with God. One good way to insure fidelity to that pattern
is recommended by a great spiritual teacher, the Jesuit Father
Caussade, who urged souls to keep in constant communion with
God, by means of the "Sacrament of the Present Moment."
His startling and revealing phrase focuses attention on the
twofold truth that wherever I am, God is; and that I shall
receive His grace at every moment and in every place, if my
mind and will are properly disposed. Holding this truth in
memory, and trying to do first things first, I may even become
a sort of humble imitation of a saint.

Again we remind ourselves that order on the lower level may
be disorder when viewed from a higher level — for example,

the careful arrangements of a brain surgeon, preparing an exceedingly dangerous operation: "All in order?" he asks. "All in order, sir," replies his assistant. "Not yet," interrupts the patient; "I must first see a priest." For the patient is most concerned not with technical order, but with order on the highest possible level, which regulates the direct relationship between his soul and God. Once more we recall that all superficial patterns of order are essential disorder, unless in harmony with God's will. Such a pattern of conduct may at first sight seem too intricate to follow. But upon reflection, we perceive that this rule of life is extremely simple — not easy, to be sure, but simple. We have only to conform to God's will, insofar as we know it. We keep going along carefully, as if we were using a flashlight, or a Geiger counter, asking at each moment, "Is this next step in accord with God's will as indicated by my conscience?" Unquestionably we do live in a complex universe. Unquestionably we do face many small and at least a few extremely difficult, problems. But essentially they all reduce to this one question: "What seems to be God's will for me here and now?" I am not obliged to seek mathematical certainty, or to wait for an infallible decision on each small question which presents itself. I must do my best to ascertain the truth and then go ahead confidently.

PEACE

Our Lord used the word "peace" many times. The Church, in her liturgy, repeats it over and over again; and when her children pass into eternity she prays, "May they rest in peace." Thus she expresses her hope that they will receive all that is needed to make them supremely, everlastingly happy; for peace means just that — the end of all suffering, the rich reward of all striving, perfect tranquillity.

Peace implies that nothing is "going wrong"; that there is neither present trouble, nor any prospect of trouble — none whatever. Here on earth peace prevails if everything in the universe is functioning properly, if nature, mankind, the invisible world are co-ordinating their activities. One could hardly hope for all this; yet spiritual peace implies even more. Not only does it exclude present disturbance and anxiety about the future — a negative sort of thing; but it gives us a solid, positive basis for expecting *perfect* happiness. That is what our Lord promised His disciples; that is what the Church asks for her children. Difficult to attain? Yes! Obtainable in this life? No! Yet not a future impossibility! For our Lord assures us that His loyal disciples will possess perfect peace in the life to come. His promise cannot be an exaggeration.

The prayer of the Church over her children is not, then, in vain. Eventually, every faithful Christian will dwell in the kingdom from which all unhappiness, all discord are excluded.

They will have fulfilled their vocation by the persevering effort to adjust their own will to God's. After having undergone whatever purification is needed, they will possess that peace which is the "tranquillity of order"; they will be remolded into God's own likeness; they will then be happy to the full measure of their capacity for happiness. This is but a way of saying that at long last each one will be a perfect lover.

When, "in the fulness of time," God actually came upon this earth, the angels welcomed Him with the song, "Peace to men" — a phrase that still re-echoes in the *Gloria,* sung or recited at daily Mass. A thrilling climax in Handel's *Oratorio* announces the Messiah as "The Prince of Peace." Turning the pages of the New Testament, we find our Lord saying, "Peace be to you!" and again, "My peace I give unto you," and still again, "Go in peace." Of His faithful followers He said, "Blessed are the peacemakers." He Himself is called "Our Peace." The kingdom of God is peace. Simeon, having fulfilled the great hope of his life, offers a prayer, *Nunc dimittis* — "Now thou dost dismiss thy servant in peace." In the apostolic teaching the first fruit of the Spirit is "peace that surpasseth all understanding."

Peace, therefore, is a most precious thing, which we must secure at any cost. What will that cost be? The question is answered in the *Imitation of Christ* which names four things that lead to great peace. Here they are: "Pray that God's plan may be perfectly fulfilled in you." "Prefer the will of another to your own." "Seek to possess less rather than more." "Always choose the lowest place." These signposts lead us along a rough road; but that is what our Lord told us to expect. It is the road He followed. His disciples follow it too.

If the prescription written by À Kempis seems too strong a dose of distasteful medicine, we had better consider carefully the consequences of rejecting it. How far shall we dare to go in doing the contrary of what the *Imitation of Christ* recommends, by giving priority to our own will, imposing it on others, seeking the lion's share for self, claiming the first place if we can? The man who devotes practically all his energy to acquiring comfort, wealth, honor, power, who is well fed, well housed, well clothed, is hardly imitating our Lord, His Mother, the apostolic Twelve, Damien the Leper, St. Francis, ill-clad and hungry, and all the men and women who through the centuries are recognized by the Church as her true children. It is only a likeness between our conduct and theirs that can set us on the road to peace. We get a stunning reminder of all this, when we recall the circumstances of the first Christmas night. Those to whom the angels brought their message of peace were poor people, lacking all the things that go with wealth and power and honor. But they were close to God.

A half century ago, an American poet, Theodosia Garrison, wrote a ballad about little cherubs playing before heaven's gate, who stared with amazement at the approach of a weary looking, shabbily dressed, dust-stained pilgrim bearing a burden but apparently anticipating a welcome to the kingdom of heaven. Then appeared an elder angel, who uttered this reproach:

> O, little foolish Cherubs,
>   What truth is this ye miss,
> There comes no saint to paradise
>   Who cometh not like this!

THE HOLY SPIRIT

I<small>T WAS</small> a startling statement that Christ made to His Apostles when He said, "It is better for you I should go away." How could it be better? Could there be any privilege preferable to that which they had enjoyed, something better than having Him as companion, teacher, friend? But Jesus repeated and explained His statement: After His going away, the Holy Spirit would come. There could be no mistake. The Gift of the Spirit was to be something more than Christ's visible Presence had been. We ponder this; and then we say, "In no other possible way could our Lord have placed greater emphasis on the truth that the visible does not equal the invisible in value." The visible Presence of Christ is surpassed by the invisible Presence of the Holy Spirit in the soul.

Our Lord's promise was fulfilled when the Apostles were assembled on the first Christian Pentecost. "Suddenly there came a sound from heaven . . . and they were all filled with the Holy Ghost." From that day onward, according to Catholic doctrine, a particular grace is bestowed upon everyone of Christ's children who receives the Sacrament of Confirmation.

When first heard, this doctrine of the Divine Indwelling seems to present a difficulty. Persons familiar with the inescapable truth that the Infinite God is omnipresent throughout the whole universe, know that He is present in the soul of every

creature — even of those who have not received the Sacrament
of Confirmation, and indeed, even of those who do not believe
in God. The seeming difficulty vanishes, when we remind
ourselves that a spirit is present wherever it is active — being
present in one fashion or another, and in a lesser or greater
degree, according to the character and the intensity of its
activity.

On the first Pentecost, according to Pope Leo XIII, God
"came not to commence His Indwelling in the souls of saints,
but to penetrate them more completely; not at that time begin-
ing to bestow His gifts, but pouring them out more abundantly;
not performing a new work, but continuing the work that He
had already begun." Just as surely as transubstantiation makes
Christ's Body present where previously it was not, just so
surely does the entrance of the Holy Spirit mean that God
Himself has come into the soul "more completely than before."
We are guilty of no exaggeration, then, when we say that the
Divine Spirit is present more intensely in a fervent than in a
tepid soul, more completely in a saint in heaven than in a
saint on earth.

St. Paul said: "You are the temple of the living God!" How
thrilling to be told that the title "temple" belongs even more
properly to the soul sanctified by the Indwelling Holy Spirit
than to the church where our Lord's Presence is marked by
the lighted sanctuary lamp! If, after our sacramental Communion, we give thanks for the physical Presence of Christ,
have we any excuse for not continuing to thank Father, Son,
and Holy Ghost, who, after the physical Presence has ceased,
still abide with us?

When we are told that the "coming" of the Holy Spirit
implies that God is present within us more actively than before,
stimulating and elevating our spiritual life, we instinctively
wish for further knowledge about this new degree of com-

panionship, this heightened possibility of co-operation between the soul and its Maker. Partly by studying our own nature and conduct, and partly by listening to competent teachers, we learn that our spiritual growth will be promoted by proper use of all those human faculties which belong to body, or mind, or will; and also by divine influence operating in all three fields. Pope Leo spoke of "secret warnings and invitations which from time to time are aroused in our minds and hearts by the inspiration of the Holy Ghost, without which there is no beginning of a good life, no making of progress, no winning of eternal salvation." When we are striving to follow God's lead, we sometimes experience a clarification of mind and a strengthening of will, which seem more than natural; a moment of fervor makes us suddenly docile and obedient to an impulse toward what is good even though also difficult.

Cardinal Manning warns that although we are in the state of grace, we may "make fools of ourselves" by the committing of venial sins which — like fine dust, gathering gradually upon a timepiece, slackening its motion, and destroying its precision — choke nascent good influences in the soul and gradually build up a habit that nullifies the pressure coming from the Gifts. Reading words like these, we begin to wonder if we have been living in a close, but far too loveless, relationship with the Indwelling Spirit. Have we allowed ourselves to be blinded by a cloud of other interests, to be distracted and weakened by the attempt to serve a multitude of petty, useless aims? Have we found ourselves sluggish in responding to noble instincts when the response will cost much labor or great pain? Systematic practice of exercise is typical of artists, musicians, athletes. The superbly trained fingers of a pianist — Paderewski, for example — give warning of a certain decline of flexibility, if daily practice is omitted even once. The saints are like that. Surely we cannot assume that without much labor *we* shall succeed in making our selfish, sluggish wills harmonize with God's divine inspirations.

As for the seven Gifts of the Spirit, merely to name them is to light up the pattern of conduct which Christians must follow. We are to cultivate habits of Wisdom, Understanding, Counsel, Knowledge, Fortitude, Piety, Fear of the Lord. A good look at them conveys a fresh conception of the soul's need of God's Presence and of His purpose in coming to us. He plants within us a latent force which with proper care will develop various forms of spiritual energy. Virtuous habits grow strong with exercise. We see the road more clearly. Our courage dominates every nascent fear, yet never leads us to the madness of pitting our strength against the strength of God.

Most comprehensive of the seven Gifts is Wisdom. As its very name suggests, it places the soul in contact with Reality; and consequently it seems to involve possession of the other Gifts. Wisdom is the quality that men look for first and cherish most in a teacher, or a leader — again, no doubt, partly because it has a suggestion of implying many powers. "Seat of Wisdom" is one of the titles applied to our Lady. It reflects our belief that she is closer to God than any other creature. When we are begging God for help at the beginning of our devotions, or during the prayers which commonly precede a sermon or conference, we ask that He will give us wisdom — *recta sapere* — that is to say, that He will enable us "to appreciate the right things." It seems a fairly comprehensive request.

If we were to analyze the nature of each of the seven Gifts and then go over the daily opportunities we have to use them, we might make more than one practically helpful discovery. Any Christian who is trying to adjust himself to the divine order by living a "godly" life here on earth is, of course, influenced by the three theological virtues — faith, hope, and charity — to believe, to trust, and to love wholeheartedly. He is further strengthened in his way of living when he receives the seven-fold Gifts. The four first named influence the mind to seek truth more clearly, to appreciate the proper value of each human act more correctly, to perceive the implications and consequences of this or that line of conduct, and to hold these things fast in memory. Of the other three Gifts, Fortitude keeps us from being deterred by any obstacle from moving along the orderly path that corresponds to God's will; whereas Fear, on the other hand, instills in us an unconquerable repugnance to disobeying God. The gift of Piety seems to be so named because it corresponds to the childlike love which our Lord pointed out as an essential characteristic of His disciples.

Thus, then, we may break down into their specific qualities the fundamental virtues that keep us in tune with the will of God, that adjust our speaking and our thinking and our doing to the orderly pattern of conduct designed for us. If we acquire these qualities, we shall be moving steadily toward the perfection of the saints — not easily, not quickly, but at least with confidence that we know the height we have to reach and that we are on our way. We are in partnership with God.

If we are inclined to shrink from employing the word *partnership* in connection with God, we should consider that this usage is as old as our English language. Juliana of Norwich wrote down, nearly six hundred years ago, that God would make us "partners" of His good deed. We should note further that we are God's partners not only in the doing of things supernatural, but even in every single thing we do. If the word *partnership* implies the co-operation of two agents in an enterprise to which each makes a contribution, then I may joyously affirm that literally I am His partner in all my activities. Both partners are active when I am resisting temptation, when I practice charity, when I walk, or talk, or even when I breathe. Our Lord's own words declare that He is always beside us, within us, helping us to do good and to avoid evil. He says: "I shall be with you always." "I am in the midst of you." "Without Me you can do nothing." We think of His admonition, "Separated from Me, you have no power to do anything." We consider St. Paul's bold declaration, "I can do all things in Him who strengthens Me."

Traveling together is a great test of friendship; for travelers are partners in an enterprise which forces them to make many decisions in common. If I am to be God's loyal partner, I must agree with Him. The more I learn about the saints, the plainer it becomes to me that they were His loyal partners. They affirmed that it was only because God carried the major part of the burden that they were able to do the things which won the admiration of man. Success in great deeds comes surely to persons who have learned to co-operate with God, not sentimentally, but wholeheartedly. That comforting truth encourages us weak mortals to undertake what otherwise we would never dare attempt.

All this must have been in St. Paul's mind when he wrote, "Whatever you do, whether you eat, or drink, or whatever else you do, do all to the glory of God" — words that throw new light on the whole texture of each day. Like him, we are never alone. I do nothing unaided — not even eating or drinking or sleeping; not walking or talking; not working or playing. My invisible partner is always at hand. If I could remain, even dimly, aware of that "Presence not to be put by," I might even achieve the habit of constant prayer.

A person once said, "When I think of myself as in partnership with our Lord, I fancy that I am like an oarsman, rowing on one side of the boat, while our Lord rows on the other. He can always be counted on; He never misses a stroke; but when I fail — and I do sometimes — the boat spins around and around in danger of drifting down into the rapids." The picture suggests what God has taught us, that His plan will not be carried out unless we co-operate. He requests; He commands; He assists; He foretells reward for obedience, and punishment for disobedience. There He leaves it. He offers me a precious privilege; and His offer involves my grave responsibility. I must face the fact that my own co-operation is indispensably necessary to the carrying out of His plan for my welfare. Unless I use my free will to co-operate in the divine plan, this plan will be to that extent frustrated.

One way in which my divine Partner aids me is by focusing a strong light upon dark stretches of road that I must traverse, by making plain certain signposts which otherwise I might not see. Sometimes He helps me — as no one else could — to realize that the example given me by others is bad example, that their advice is unsafe to follow. Later, at the end of an episode — I perceive how wonderfully I have been aided and I see the danger, or the failure, that has been narrowly avoided. Sometimes again the voice of my Partner bids me beware lest I give bad example to my neighbor, lest I paint scandalous pictures by my carelessness and selfishness, thus casting discredit on my faith, thus building lying beacons on a perilous shore and causing shipwrecks. I have my Partner to thank for recalling me to my senses, saving me from foolish decisions and from reckless choice of companions and of amusements. In how many ways would I be far less happy and much more sinful than I am, but for God's restraining hand and His words of warning whispered quietly in my conscience.

If, then, I hesitate about responding to a good inspiration, if I draw back from the undertaking of a difficult duty, if I dally with temptations to be uncharitable, or resentful, or rashly inquisitive, I should remind myself of what will happen — my boat will spin around and around, and drift downstream, maybe to the falls!

BELIEVING

Dictionaries give a variety of meanings to the word "faith." The Catholic uses the word to describe something far different from a "feeling" that something is true. Faith is not, as some persons imagine, a credulous acceptance without adequate motive, a comfortable attitude of mind that excludes fear of future hardship or suffering. Neither does faith consist of oral recitation of a prescribed formula, or of many formulas. Nor is it exact theological knowledge, nor intellectual appreciation of abstract truth, nor ability to answer difficult questions. What is it then?

Theologians describe faith as assent to a statement based on the testimony of another. If that other is a human being, we have "human faith"; if that other is God, we have "divine faith." When truth is revealed by God and communicated by the Church, assent to it is called "Catholic faith." The degree of perfection in our faith varies from person to person; for it depends in large measure on the correspondence of the will to God's helping grace. Perfect faith implies an unreserved wholehearted acceptance — the believer will die rather than give up the Faith. A saint who is no scholar may have perfect faith. A child's faith may be more nearly perfect than the faith of an intellectual genius. Sometimes an odious sense is given to the phrase "seeing is believing." Nevertheless, in a very true and proper sense, we may say, "To believe is to see" — that is, the eyes of the soul may see what cannot be seen by the eyes of the body.

A few years ago, a newly ordained priest, who had been a Protestant minister, chose for his first sermon the text: "Blessed are the eyes that see the things which you see." In the circumstances, it seemed to be the most fitting text that could have been selected. The sermon stirred the hearers with a remembrance of visions that faith reveals — of our divine Lord Himself; of the ever present, infinitely loving Father; of the fairest of all creatures, Mary Immaculate. They saw in the distance our Lord teaching, healing, winning, sanctifying those with whom He came in contact; and they realized that everyone who has the gift of faith shares to some extent the blessing of Christ's own disciples, who, living in a sort of earthly paradise, associating with Jesus daily, looking at the world through God's eyes, perceived so clearly the path, narrow but straight, which leads to eternal life. That sermon must have made many of its hearers resolve — as even the mention of it may now make us resolve — to read the Gospel more frequently and attentively, to picture its various scenes more vividly, to absorb its spirit more fervently. For the Gospel conveys lessons that are among man's most precious heirlooms. It reveals a world which is properly God's own kingdom — inhabited by persons varying from one another in many details, persons of different origins, social, intellectual, and spiritual, yet displaying an amazing degree of likeness — all made one by their oneness of faith. Through the eyes of faith we see how superlatively meek, forgiving, chaste, obedient we should be. These are the things, the sight of which makes us blessed.

And we also see that — despite certain extraordinary notions cherished by the uninformed — Catholic life is not fitted into a complete pattern of minute details devised by the Church and imposed upon the conscience of the believer. The main outlines of unity are imparted by revelation; they are interpreted by the Church divinely commissioned to interpret them and to impose disciplinary obedience in God's name. Outside of this essential core, there are beliefs and practices cherished by some, but not by others; forms of devotion prized highly in certain regions and during certain centuries, but less highly in other regions and other centuries. Like the created universe, the world of faith presents variety; yet there is not, and never can be, disunity with regard to fundamentals. Here again, spiritual life resembles physical life. Without air, heat, food, the body and the mind will perish. The grace of God keeps the soul spiritually alive; it must be nourished by faith and good deeds. If we do not look at, think about, act in harmony with the truths communicated by God, this neglect will entail spiritual decay — a sad fact often exemplified by the disintegration of persons provided with splendid opportunities, who conform to the externals of belief for years, but finally fall, as a secretly diseased human body collapses.

"Blessed are the eyes that see the things which you see." Catholics — but comparatively few others — understand the full meaning of this. One Catholic mother showed that she understood it when she said, "I would rather have my children unable to read and write than uninstructed in their faith." She knew that faith gives life to the soul; that the will plays an indispensable part in preserving the soul's life; and that to save the life of the soul, the martyrs gladly gave up the life of the body.

A curious phenomenon, called "psychic blindness," occurs at times both in human beings and in lower animals. On these occasions optical vision remains as before; but the normal recognition of things is lacking; the power of interpreting has been lost. A bird may walk into the jaws of a cat; a man may look at his intimate friends and relatives, without realizing who they are; or he may venture into deadly peril unawares. This condition recalls the state of a soul blind to the reflection of

God's qualities in the world — in the beauty of sunset and evening star, in a mother's self-forgetting heroism, in the holiness of a saint. Such blindness may be cured, however, if those afflicted will repeatedly focus their attention on objects which, in "sacramental" fashion, suggest divine things hidden within. We are not always able to see beneath the surface of tree and flower, or beyond the "clouds that gather round the setting sun"; but, then again, at times some special gift of vision is granted:

> Yet ever and anon a trumpet sounds
> From the hid battlements of Eternity;
> Those shaken mists a space unsettle, then
> Round the half-glimpsed turrets slowly wash again.

HOPING

Some playful spirit once suggested that a sort of Ninth Beatitude might be: "Blessed are those who expect nothing; they shall not be disappointed." The jest conveys a profound truth. At long last, persons who hope for *nothing* will have precisely that — nothing. Whereas those who trust confidently in God's goodness, will, despite misfortune, injustice, hardship, and past repented sins, possess at the end perfect peace, trust, joy.

In an ever memorable moment, St. Paul wrote to the disciples in Rome, "We are saved by hope!" What other words could so forcibly convey the truth that grace does not run counter to fine human aspirations; it does not destroy nature; it fits into and harmonizes with every good quality! By being a hopeful Christian, one becomes a better man or woman, a wiser father or mother, a happier friend, a finer citizen.

Hope is a sort of forgotten virtue. Few of us remember that it is one of the three supereminent habits which make the soul dear to God. Do we not stress the importance of faith and love at the expense of hope? Do not persons who are sensitive with regard to sins against faith and charity often overlook the duty of examining conscience for possible offenses against hope? Do we not seem to think we can be saved without hoping, although we cannot be saved without believing and loving? In plain words, is not hope treated like the proverbial stepchild or poor relation?

It is, then, a duty to cultivate hope. Further, we must keep from destroying or weakening hope, either in our own souls or in the souls of our neighbors. Just as we are bound to refrain from thinking or saying or reading what will injure faith or charity, so, too, we are bound to shun what would discourage hope. We even have a further positive obligation to think and act in a way that will foster hope.

A common obstacle to the development of hope is the habit of idly drifting down the current of thoughts which suggest anxiety or fear. This danger will be avoided only if we are willing to try and try and try again to substitute carefully selected objects of thought for those which impose themselves upon us. Instead of letting our little boat float downstream, we must paddle against the current, not straining, yet persistently putting forth a reasonable degree of exertion.

Hope, like every other virtue, is essentially active; it often involves a pushing aside of formidable obstacles; it may imply, perhaps, heroic persistence. But it rests upon the sound theological teaching that God will never demand from me anything that is beyond my power. Duty is never impossible — difficult maybe, but never impossible. The virtue of hope implies that I am doing *my best* — but unless I am really doing my best, really trying to perform my duty, I possess neither faith nor hope nor charity.

Hope, then, can no more be associated with indifference to God's will than it can be separated from faith and love. The three virtues are co-ordinated activities; they interlock; they affect one another; they grow strong or weak together. Despair, which excludes hope, is incompatible with true faith and true love. We must not forget the fundamental principle impressed upon the young theologian: "To one who does what in him lies, God never refuses grace." If I do all that I can do to please God, He will not exclude me from heaven.

Physicians dissuade patients from too much attention to their own symptoms; spiritual teachers bid us avoid excessive introspection. A retreat master once observed that a person who keeps looking continually into a mirror will probably find definite reasons to feel discouraged. These warnings about what not to do give a clue to what we should do — namely, look outward and upward; keep our mind fastened upon God; reflect upon our Saviour's words and deeds. If we fill our souls with the things of God, we shall forget self in large measure. What a striking lesson on the virtue of hope we find in St. Matthew's story of St. Peter walking upon the water — safely until he became afraid, and then no longer safely. When our Lord, answering his cry for help, stretched forth His hand, and rescued him, He also uttered the reproach, "Why didst thou doubt, O thou of little faith?"

It is no news that a man is at his best when he is hopeful. This is the principle acted upon by a football coach who gives a "pep" talk to his team between halves; by an impresario encouraging his protégé to walk bravely out upon the stage; by a doctor who says to the patient's family, "The real trouble is that he *thinks* he cannot get well. Put hope in his heart and he will soon be on his feet again." This is in line with Catholic teaching on the important role of hope in spiritual progress — an illustration of the general truth that grace complements and elevates nature. We must remember that the development of a virtue depends not merely on God's gift of grace to us, but also on our state of mind and will. If confident, relaxed, hopeful, we may progress; if depressed, frightened, fearful, we probably stand still, or fall back. How often we note, either in ourselves or in others, that self-consciousness gives rise to hopelessness; and that the anticipated failure is followed by the actual failure. This does not mean that spiritual achievement is solely a wish, an aspiration, but rather that in pursuing perfection we cannot expect to get something for nothing. Salvation is not a reward of

> Something noble and wise and good,
> Done by merely wishing we could.

Obviously, it is absurd to say that a man can do whatever he wishes to do; or to say that, if determined, he will surely overcome every obstacle that opposes his attainment of a cherished ambition. It is true, however, that he will profit by every experience, no matter how painful, if he is co-operating with the grace of God. The Church has always taught — against two types of heretical contradiction — that nothing created by God is evil, and that good will can use all things as helps to salvation. The patient endurance of the martyrs amid their agonizing torments, and the less heroic, yet difficult, acceptance of hardship by the typical Catholic register belief in this truth.

The form of religion commonly known as "Christian Science" is a distortion of the doctrine just outlined. That the false doctrine bears some resemblance to the true was made plain by the priest who announced a sermon on the virtue of hope as a talk on "Catholic Christian Science." But there is also a wide difference. For, although both accept St. Paul's principle, "To those who love God, all things work together for good," the Catholic goes on to proclaim the high spiritual value of pain, whereas the "Scientist" denies the very existence of pain: "It it a mere delusion of your sinful self. You have no toothache; you merely think you have, because you are a sinner." The truth is that, although you are suffering from a really aching tooth, the pain cannot hinder you from attaining joy. Indeed, if endured in the right spirit, it will further your progress toward happiness. This is the true meaning of St. Paul's saying; and this is a sound basis for practicing the virtue of hope, always and everywhere.

LOVING

Years ago a young novice came upon a book with the promising title, *The Greatest Thing in the World*. To his chagrin, however, the book when opened proved to be a mere discussion of charity; and his reaction was, "Oh! Is that all!" He had made a hasty judgment. The book was actually an inspiring comment on one of the most famous passages in literature, which opens with St. Paul's warning to the Corinthians: "If I speak with the tongues of men, and of angels, and have not charity, I am become as sounding brass." After many years spent in studying the ups and downs of life, the novice, by this time grown old, affirmed emphatically that he no longer questioned the fitness of the title. He said, "Charity is indeed the greatest thing in the world."

The subject of charity may be approached from so many angles that one faces a bewildering choice. Perhaps we had best begin by recalling that charity is one of the three supreme virtues, named theological, or unitive, because they unite the soul with God. By faith we believe; by hope we trust; by charity we give ourselves. Charity is distinctly and emphatically the greatest of these three. Faith is the virtue by means of which we believe in God; therefore, in heaven, where we see God — no more faith! And hope is the virtue by which we expect heaven; therefore after having reached heaven — no more

39

hope! When faith and hope have done their work, charity, the virtue by which we give ourselves to God, reigns alone. *Sola regnat caritas.* "Charity never falleth away." Loving God with all our strength, totally, unconditionally, unreservedly, and for His sake, loving all other beings, we forever resemble Him.

If we examine the etymology of the word "charity," we see its relation to the Latin word *carus* (dear). An old lay Sister, noted for her patience, once said that, eighteen years earlier, a retreat master had drawn attention to the relation between these two words and had suggested that a good way to cultivate charity would be to try to act like "a perfect dear" toward everybody all the time. The old lay Sister added that for eighteen years she had been trying to do just that. It was a big order. But she seemed to be filling it nobly.

We get a new notion of the large content of charity, if we realize what is involved in being "a perfect dear" to everybody all the time. For this implies that we take a loving attitude not only toward "nice" people, but also toward mean, "nasty" people — persons who have been unkind and unjust to us, who have made us suffer greatly, whose very name when mentioned excites violent emotions. Of certain individuals, I may be tempted to say, "I never want to hear his name mentioned again"; or "She is the one person I could never forgive." Yet if I have charity, I cannot willfully speak, or think, or act that way toward anyone. The temptation may be extremely difficult to resist; but I must make the heroic choice. If I have not charity, I am as "sounding brass," and I cannot qualify for heaven.

This lofty doctrine comes from the highest possible authority. On one occasion, our Lord addressed His disciples in these words: "What credit is it to you, if you love those who love you? Even sinners love those who love them. . . . It is your enemies you must love." If that seems to be a hard saying — as it certainly is — if we need reassurance that our Lord meant literally the words just quoted, then we have only to remember the plea He made for His executioners while He was dying upon the cross: "Father, forgive them, for they know not what they do."

To get into heaven, one must be like our Lord; to be like our Lord, one must be divinely kind and gentle toward the mean, the cruel, the brutal, even toward those who inexcusably and unreasonably dislike us. We must pray, "Father, forgive them; they did not know what they were doing, when they treated me like that." Am I ready now to speak these words?

Let us make no mistake about it. If charity were the common practice of all mankind — or even of those men and women who inherit and profess the ideals that the Church has cherished through the ages — the world would be literally transformed. But whether I picture the great world with its two billion people, or consider the behavior merely of those who come under my observation day by day, I find an almost terrifying contrast between the conduct of the average Christian and the ideals preached and personified by our blessed Lord. These ideals seem as far removed from our daily experience and from our own habitual way of thinking as fairy tales. And if I am shocked by the difference between the profession and the conduct of my neighbors, I may receive a much more devastating shock when I look into my own soul. Noting my — more or less unconscious — reaction toward many persons with whom I come in frequent contact, I see how lightly I am taking Christ's words. For I am not devoting my best energies to the reproducing of His life in mine. In fact, I seem not really to believe that Christians must be gracious and generous and affectionate toward persons who are disagreeable or rude or mean. But if I don't believe that, then I don't really believe that "the man who dislikes his neighbor is displeasing to God."

I must face this issue frankly, sum it up simply. Do I,

or do I not, act as if I believed that to shut out my enemies, will be to shut Christ out also — that God Himself will not enter a heart from which love of enemies is excluded? Perhaps it would be a profitable spiritual exercise for me this very day, first to list the persons I like least, and then to note how I behave toward them.

II.

GOD WITH US

THE Old Testament carries the reader as far as the Maccabean Wars and the Roman occupation of Judea. The story of the Jews comes to an end about a century before the birth of Christ; then the New Testament tells us about the fulfillment of the ancient prophecies and the coming of the Messiah, born in the little town of Bethlehem — in the year 785, according to the Roman calendar, which corresponds to the year 3760 in the Jewish calendar, and approximates the first year of the Christian era.

In the prophecies, the description of the Messiah presents a confusing alternation of glorious triumph and of abject suffering. As the latter feature had been largely lost sight of in the course of time, the humble circumstances of our Lord's birth clashed with the general anticipation of a splendid, warlike Messiah. The Son of Mary, homeless, poor, was bent on no conquest except that of winning men to love and serve the heavenly Father; and the burden of His preaching was to urge complete submission to the will of God. When seized by His enemies, He was as submissive and helpless as a convicted criminal. This contrast between what had been expected and what actually occurred led many to reject Jesus, and to denounce His Gospel as an attempt to found a new religion. In fact, however, as a careful study will show, the life of Jesus was a striking fulfillment of the messianic prophecies. The Church specifically declares that these prophecies form an essential part of Holy Scripture.

As a text for spiritual study, the New Testament has matchless value. Catholics should seek a much closer acquaintance with it than they can gather from reading, or listening to, the Sunday Gospels. Hence it seems worthwhile to suggest that all who are eager for spiritual progress should own and use a New Testament with fairly large print, a few simple maps of the New Testament lands, Hartdegan's *Harmony of the Gospels,* Newton Thompson's *Concordance to the Bible.* To these might well be added *The Saviour's Life in the Words of the Four Gospels,* edited by a Paulist Father; the valuable *Life of Christ* by Ricciotti; Prat's *Jesus Christ;* and Father Huby's recently issued *Commentary on St. Mark and St. Matthew.*

Going through the Gospels with the aid of a concordance, we can select from our Lord's own words a text for each day of the year; and we can spend a few minutes daily reflecting on the text assigned. The concordance will help us also to find passages bearing on the virtues we are particularly eager to acquire, and the defects we are trying to eliminate. Then again, if we are parents or teachers, we may try our hand at translating a Gospel episode or a parable into a story for children. For whatever purpose we use the texts, the exercise of selecting and paraphrasing them will be of benefit to us.

One who studies the New Testament intelligently acquires a fairly clear notion of the kingdom which Christ came to establish. Three ideas stand out in His Gospel: man's absolute dependence on the heavenly Father; the mutual exclusiveness of egotism and love; the divine value of pain which can so marvelously transform a selfish creature into a perfect lover. The student perceives that a sense of dependence on the Father implies not only a habit of adoring God, but also a habit of serving the neighbor for His sake, and even a readiness to overcome our human dislike of pain. Pursuing these ideals, the disciple may confidently hope to attain "The Vision" which, although dim in this life, will be truly beatific in the next. For, at long last, the soul, having learned really how to love, will be united to God in close communion for eternity.

With regard to our attitude toward God, we may learn much from a study of the words and the actions of our Lord. Repeatedly He spoke of "My Father"; "your Father"; "our Father"; "Father of all." Down through the Christian centuries, a certain primacy has attached to this title. God is our Father; we are His children. The Lord's Prayer inculcates the sentiments He wished His disciples to cherish. His words indicate the correct tone to be adopted by each one of us when we address God. A most generous Father, endowing us with life, and with many precious gifts of body and soul, God has placed us in possession of the material universe; and, on a higher level, He has enriched us with divine grace. Finite beings though we are, we may call ourselves truly His children. A relationship so intimate as to be literally breath-taking inspires our thinking, our willing, our longing. I am God's offspring, I am His child; I belong to Him more literally, more completely, than to my own father and mother.

When we recall our Lord's invitation to call the infinite God our Father, we recall also that He invited — indeed commanded — us to become like little children. Most of us, however, will admit that we pay almost no attention to the startling implication of this. Which one of us studies the qualities and characteristics of the ideal child with a view to acquire them? Which of us labors at the duty of becoming dependent, completely trustful, instinctively obedient? The "child" of the Gospel is a symbol of uncalculating affection, of readiness to trust, to obey, to follow. A disciple who is childlike will follow the Master, despite pain and even the threat of death. It is the ideal presented to us by our Lord Himself. We have free will; we may accept that ideal or reject it. But remember! Unless we are like little children, we cannot enter the kingdom of heaven.

Not long ago, the training of the child was more widely influenced by the Catholic tradition of family life, which originated in the home at Nazareth. That touchingly simple, Catholic ideal still retains sufficient vitality to produce impressive examples of moral beauty and strength; and quaint, simple habits of thought and speech still linger in truly Catholic households. But this tradition is excluded from any system of training inspired by secularism. And, since we are all to some extent at the mercy of our neighbors, the old spiritual ideal seems destined to be diluted, when not totally destroyed, by the current atmosphere which must be breathed in by both parents and children.

THE REVOLUTION

THERE is never any real contradiction between the laws of the supernatural world and the laws of the natural world; both are from God. Human beings who live in both worlds must co-ordinate the laws of both. They have to take account of the teachings of the Gospel and of the Church; and they must also adapt themselves to ascertained facts in the fields of biology and psychology. They must accept the established relationship between what is human and what is divine, between the law and the spirit.

Neglect of the stern warning of the prophets led Israel to a period of decadence. The dominant Pharisees, who placed more emphasis on the letter of the law than its spirit, devised petty rules and regulations to cover the whole field of moral and religious conduct. This attempt — necessarily doomed to failure — tended to make legal observance all important, at the expense of inner reverence and worship. Inevitably, it led to compromise. Some persons disguised their secret ambition by professing noble aims; some became cogs and robots; some ignored all external obligation and focused attention exclusively on self. On the contrary, the Gospel pattern, which is sacramental, insists both on obedience to external authority and on inner conformity to the divine will. It enunciates principles which are superlatively reasonable, and which vary greatly in their application according to circumstances. By emphasizing the double aspect of His teaching, our Lord highlighted the inevitable conflict between the Gospel and the Mosaic code, the New Law and the Old Law. St. John refers to this pointedly when he writes: "Through Moses the Law was given to us; through Jesus Christ grace came to us and truth."

The laws of the kingdom of God are unlike the majestic Roman law or the British Constitution, each of which dominated so much of the world for so many centuries. In fact, they are unlike any human code; for they deal primarily with man's inner soul, not with his external behavior. More than once in the New Testament we are told — sometimes in Christ's own words, sometimes in a passage written by one of His disciples — that love is the fulfilling of the law. The Gospel, rating outer deeds as only secondary, probes into the depths of conscience, aims to bring each least act of the will under the control of love. Whenever an individual makes a free choice, that intention, that wish must be adjusted to God's will as perceived by the individual.

Primarily and fundamentally, the Gospel is a religion of the spirit. It is not a mere specific code graven on tables of stone; yet neither does it leave us free of all external obligations. Both inner and outer life must conform to "the law of liberty" which permeates the whole being. The children of God obey at any cost; their loyalty knows no limit. The martyrs made that plain to the world.

It is questionable if most of us properly appreciate the vast influence on Christian history exercised by the record of the lives and sufferings of the saints. This is especially true in the case of the martyrs, many of whom died for the Faith, crucified or disemboweled or burned inside a brazen bull or thrown into the sea in a bag with serpents. To them the Church points, proud as the Roman matron, Cornelia, saying, "These are my children!" From the earliest times local churches kept a list of martyrs; and, when freedom came under Constantine, many of these lists were incorporated in the Roman martyrology, which eventually became part of the liturgy and is read daily during Prime.* Thus, the Church's affectionate concern for her children who have passed into eternity keeps their memory fresh in the minds of each new generation; and the story of the torments to which the martyrs were subjected stamps upon the Christian consciousness an indelible picture of the depths to which human brutality can descend and of the heights to which divine grace lifts men and women of good will.

---

* The Roman martyrology is available in an English translation, edited by Herbert Thurston, S.J.

THE KINGDOM

WHEN our Lord, in His Sermon on the Mount, proclaimed the Beatitudes, He established a kingdom committed to everlasting war against the kingdom of the world. His declaration must have seemed like a promise that water would run uphill, that the sun would rise in the west, or at least that a quiet word would drown out the yells of excited mobs. Love was to be the only badge of citizenship, the one patent of nobility. Ideals were personified by the poor, the meek, the humble, the patient. It seemed to be a confusing, depressing, impossible pattern. The average listener could hardly help recalling that normal men look for rewards visible, tangible, soothing to nature, and that our Lord's ideals run counter to man's dominant egotism. We seek possession, power, freedom from care; we follow selfish pursuits, disregarding obstacles set up by justice and truth and mercy and peace, and even the will of God. We hunger for things that make us comfortable. We may talk about the trying lot of persons ill-fed, ill-clothed, ill-housed; yet few of us are wholehearted in helping them, and many of us ignore or discourage them, and even repel and insult them. How slow we are to welcome even-handed justice when it runs counter to our own interests; to look upon costly peace as preferable to cheap dissension and quarreling. How much we resemble those worldly-minded hearers, who remained untouched as our Lord was formulating ideals which would remain valid in every age; would evoke a heroic response not matched by any other in all human history; and would show how souls softened by suffering absorb God's grace more readily than souls wrapped in habits of self-indulgence. Theoretically at least, we recognize this. Not only do we honor the martyrs in our prayers; we take pride in giving their names to our children. We hardly do this in the hope the little ones will become rich, popular, and famous. If that were our main purpose, there would be no point in using the names of any one of the Apostles or of the saints commemorated in the Canon of the Mass or of the *Mater Dolorosa,* whose Son was destined to suffer and die for justice' sake.

As described in the Sermon on the Mount, the word "blessed" includes two types of persons. First come those commonly regarded as unfortunate, because they lack things which most human beings expect, or at least desire, to possess; these persons may be called the "Have Nots." The second type includes persons who commonly spend most of their time and energy in prayer and in serving God and their neighbors; these persons are the "Givers."

It seems safe to assume that when our Lord spoke on the hillside, He was addressing a crowd among which were many "Have Nots," many poor persecuted, oppressed souls, hardly able to keep from grieving because of their misfortunes. It was persons of this sort whom He declared to be blessed. Can it be that, in spite of what He said, you and I are inclined to doubt that it is fortunate to belong to one of the classes just named? If so, we had better consider our spiritual situation very carefully.

Another type of "blessed," not commonly held in high honor, are "the meek." The word seems to be the equivalent of "spiritless." But if we read over the dictionary synonyms for "meek," we come upon such words as "mild-tempered," "not easily provoked," "patient under injuries," "not vain or haughty, or resentful." Or, again, we meet "long-suffering," "yielding," "pacific," "not domineering, blustering, or fretful." The meekness of which our Lord speaks is the kind of meekness which harmonizes a Christian's will with the will of the heavenly Father. The moral strength of the saint, his truly powerful personality, quickly come into play if anyone tries to persuade him to lower his spiritual ideals for the sake of worldly advantage or social approval. Then he is wholly unyielding. This is the kind of meekness which you and I must acquire if we are to apply for admission into the kingdom of heaven.

A statement which needs special attention is our Lord's declaration: "Blessed are those who suffer persecution for justice' sake." These are persons who have gained control over the normal impulses which bid us resent instantly and strongly whatever seems to be discourteous or unjust. Sometimes emotion sweeps us off our feet without warning, giving us no time to think; and we "jump the gun." When our dignity or rights seem to be attacked, instantaneous reaction breaks out in violent words or deeds. As only seasoned troops can be trusted to stand still under fire, so only promising candidates for high places in heaven can be depended upon to resist the impact of unpleasant events and depressing failures. These blessed ones seem to be but half aware of what is going on, because they are inwardly busy fitting distasteful experience into God's providential plan. "The patience of a saint" has become a proverb. But, as for me, I must still ask myself: "Does an attack on my rights or my dignity usually evoke a show of moral strength, or of moral weakness?"

We may find it difficult at first to understand why our Lord classifies as "blessed" the persons who grieve. He is, however, not referring to prophets of gloom, who look always upon the dark side and always forecast the worst. The "blessed" are those who mourn as our Lord mourned at the tomb of Lazarus, as our Lady mourned at the foot of the cross. They are essentially sympathetic, nobly human. They can be bowed down by grief; but they are never crushed or broken in spirit, never hysterical, never despairing. Theirs is the measure of a hero. Tyrants may be able to kill such a man's body; they can never destroy his soul. No man, no demon can interrupt his peaceful communion with God. He is indeed blessed!

Now, the "Givers." They are lovers of justice. They are the men and women who, at great cost to themselves, assist and protect the alien, the helpless, the sinful. They are the persons who never — absolutely never — condemn anyone unless he is proven guilty, no matter what pressure is brought to bear. Are we of this class? Do we advocate justice when it will imply a loss of income or popularity, when it menaces the material welfare of ourselves, our friends, our country?

To "give" is, of course, an essential attribute of love. We look upon the saints as the greatest lovers that the world has ever seen, because of their unlimited generosity in giving to God — and for His sake to the neighbor — everything they possessed, everything they could hope to possess. In a sense it may be said that religion is summed up in giving — that is, in giving everything to God, to whom alone it is lawful to give everything. I shall not be fit for heaven until I have learned to do this. If I have not learned it before death, then, provided I am patient, I shall learn the art in purgatory and practice it in heaven. Only when I make God's will mine, when I reserve nothing for myself, only then shall my soul be sufficiently like Him to be admitted into His presence, to possess Him for eternity.

If we go through the whole long story of renunciations practiced by our Lord's followers down the ages, we get new light about the inner nature of holiness and about the far-reaching implications of the words our Lord spoke on the Mount or at the lakeside. We see so clearly that love is not properly measured by the rigor of the renunciation or by the kind of heroism practiced, but by the inner giving up of the will, by the total "abandonment" of which Caussade speaks. Saints are souls who have given all to God. They have made the gift in diverse ways. Our Blessed Lady and the Apostles followed patterns of conduct superficially different, yet essentially the same. Being lovers, they were "givers," who never counted the cost, never calculated the reward. Fortunate is the Catholic who keeps in memory the record of all these heroic, perfect lovers, the meaning of whose conduct is made plain by the teaching Church.

It is good to be familiar with the ways in which saints give everything to God; it is also good at times to concentrate attention upon some individual saint, whose particular pattern of giving makes a special impression upon us. Thus we may profitably recall the heroic Jesuit, Peter Claver, who, in his own words, made himself "slave of the Negro slaves." In nauseating conditions, too horrible to describe, he devoted himself for more than forty years to the physical and spiritual assistance of the poor creatures shipped from Africa to Cartagena to be sold in that chief slave market of the New World. His patient gentleness, his heroic attention to all their needs so won the confidence of these unhappy people that before he died, he had instructed and baptized more than three hundred thousand of them.

Another princely giver was *Il Poverello*, that "poor little fellow" of Assisi, whose character has cast a spell over the world for some six centuries, arousing admiration and affection in all types of men and women. To many, he is the disciple of Christ who best reflects the characteristics of the Master.

All in all, history seems to affirm that the "impossible" ideals of the Sermon on the Mount actually work.

THE LAST SUPPER

THE scene in the Upper Room at the Last Supper reminds us almost irresistibly of the beginning of our Lord's earthly life in Bethlehem. For at the Last Supper began that mysterious sacramental life which keeps Christ ever present on this earth until the end of time. Since then He lives with us in the consecrated Bread and Wine which are His Body and Soul, His humanity and divinity. From the Upper Room a little group of humble persons, radiant with gratitude for the heavenly Father's divine Gift, went forth to devote their lives to spreading the message of Christ to all the world even at the cost of martyrdom. In fact, the Last Supper might well be called a sort of forecast of the Church's life throughout the centuries, with good and evil, strength and weakness, faith and treachery, holiness and sacrilege closely associated. Da Vinci found in that scene inspiration for one of the greatest pictures ever painted; and he was successful in conveying so much of its beauty and significance that by common acknowledgment his work has been ranked among the greatest artistic achievements of all time. Even his unfinished sketches are still carefully treasured.

To the Church and to her children, the Last Supper, like the Crucifixion, remains an essential element of the Faith. Over each of her buildings she places a cross beneath which, on the altar, takes place the central act of worship, a continuation of the Last Supper, enacted in obedience to Christ's words: "Do this in commemoration of Me." At Mass sometimes, or during a procession of the Blessed Sacrament when the echoes of the *Pange Lingua* are rolling through the aisles of a great church, one seems to recapture the atmosphere of that Upper Room where Jesus and the Twelve gathered for their last Paschal meal, and where the shadow of approaching gloom vanished as our Lord bestowed the Gift promised long before — the Gift, so incredibly magnificent that, as St. John relates, certain fainthearted disciples could not even bring themselves to believe in it. It would not be strange if every time I witness a priest using Christ's own words to transform bread and wine into His Body and Blood, all the long centuries of Christian worship should seem to meet in my soul and deepen the fervor with which I say, *"Adoro te!"*

It is, of course, literally impossible to describe the general and lasting response of human hearts to our Lord's Gift of Himself in Holy Communion. History records nothing that even faintly resembles the outpouring of grateful devotion that has come from men and women and little children during the centuries since that Gift was first made. An ideal stimulus to adoration, the Real Presence gives a unique quality to the church where Holy Mass has been celebrated, or where the Blessed Sacrament is reserved in the tabernacle. Sorrow for sin — the minimum qualification for a peaceful death — is also the necessary condition for a worthy Holy Communion; and the sense of having been thus prepared becomes a new incentive to fervent gratitude. The least sentimental soul is stirred when approaching the altar rail for Communion, or even when kneeling as the Blessed Sacrament is carried in procession among worshiping crowds. Men, women, and children at the altar rail, or in the pews, look at the face that still reflects the radiance of Thabor, the agony of Gethsemani, the shame of

Calvary. They listen to the words of pardon which still welcome each penitent sinner, longing to receive the Bread of Life that gives strength to famishing souls. Each one of us belongs to this worshiping multitude. Each one of us when we approach Holy Communion, or give thanks afterward, is communing with our Saviour, heeding His admonitions, promising him whole-hearted fidelity, and repudiating forever habits which have destroyed, or weakened, our intimacy with Him.

It is good at times to remember that our Communion is not intended to be a merely transient relationship. On that great day in the synagogue at Capharnaum when Jesus foretold what would occur at the Last Supper, He used a word much favored in the Gospel — saying, "He that eateth My flesh and drinketh My blood *abideth* in Me and I in him." The word is significant, because it seems to stress the lasting character of that indwell-ing; and, indeed, the very idea of bread implies that it does not serve its essential purpose by being consumed. As bread is assimilated in order to become a source of health and strength, contributing to every activity of body and mind, so with the spiritual nourishment effected by Holy Communion. This is the keynote for our response to our Lord's announcement of His Gift at the Last Supper. Our thanksgiving, our worship, should be lasting. Our Lord gives Himself, not for a moment or an hour or a day, but for life, for eternity. So it is only by means of a lifelong habit of thanksgiving, filled with countless renewals of faith and adoration, that we can make fitting acknowledgment. This is why Communion, remembered and repeated, exercises a strengthening and purifying effect, raising us to a level where adoration is a habit rather than an act, a state of soul rather than a brief experience. Our Lord abides in me and I in Him. This helps me to understand why and how each new sacramental Communion, like each new prayer, deepens that union of my soul with its Maker, which began when grace was first bestowed on me, and which, unless I forfeit it, will continue to grow until it fills the whole capacity of my soul. Then, at last, man will have become sufficiently Godlike to enjoy the Beatific Vision. I shall see Him as He is.

All this seems to enlighten us as to the type of prayer we should use when preparing for Communion or when making our thanksgiving. Our prayer should have an "abiding" quality. It should be an endless, depthless, giving of self which, beginning as a transient act, gives promise of developing into habitual, uninterrupted love. Some of the soul-stirring phrases used in the liturgy and many of the simple aspirations favored by the saints convey a suggestion of the tone and temper of their communion with God. It would not be without value for us to fashion a sort of small private prayer book of our own, for use before or after Communion. In it we might register phrases that we have assimilated from books and others that we have ourselves devised. These latter, just because they are our own, may well prove to be more helpful, even if less striking and poetic, than those that can be found in books. As to helpful sources for the discovery of our aspirations, we may turn to the New Testament and also — perhaps next — to Book IV of *The Imitation of Christ* where we are bidden to realize the "great reverence" with which Christ is to be received; the depth of "God's great goodness and charity in this Sacrament"; the need we have to "offer ourselves and all that is ours, to God." Other sources are literally too numerous to mention. For the moment we may recall the rich suggestiveness of liturgical hymns and of some others written for popular use. And then, of course, there are the brief aspirations associated with the names of St. Thomas the Apostle, St. Peter, St. Augustine, St. Patrick, St. Thomas Aquinas, St. Ignatius. Indeed, the devout soul has close at hand an inexhaustible mine of suggestions for the making of private prayer.

THE ROYAL ROAD

THE Crucifixion of our Lord came at the end of a painful journey along what we call the *Via Dolorosa*. The journey is now commemorated in that greatly loved devotion, the Stations of the Cross — which forms an integral part of Catholic devotion during Lent and Holy Week, and especially on Good Friday. It enables us to accompany our Lord on His painful journey; we seem to feel what He felt during His three falls; we almost hear Him speaking to His Blessed Mother, to Veronica, to the weeping women of Jerusalem. And when the soldiers strip Him of His garments and nail Him to the cross and lift Him up before the crowd, we hear that last message which repeats and sums up the lessons He had earlier imparted to His disciples.

Few words are more solemn than those of a dying man, above all when they come from the lips of a leader who is directing his disciples how to avoid future perils. Ever since they were uttered, the words of Jesus have provided His followers with subjects of meditation and with texts for sermons. We dwell upon them with confident assurance that they will aid our progress on the path that leads to holiness. This was in the mind of the author of that incomparable booklet, *The Imitation of Christ,* who, five or six centuries ago, wrote, "There is no other way to hope and peace than the royal way of the holy cross."

Pondering our Lord's first Word, we remember how strongly
He urges all who would be His disciples to show good will
to every man and to shun hatred as a thing that comes from
the Evil One. It is when the appalling shout of joy comes from
the lips of His enemies as He is lifted up on the cross to
which He has been nailed that we hear Him say: "Father,
forgive them." To us these words give certainty that from
that moment onward forever, the spirit of hate will never again
triumph over the spirit of love. Hate may blaspheme God,
torment the just, crucify the saints — but no more. And eventually it will be cast out and annihilated — proof that love is
unconquerable, immortal, divine.

We remember what Christ said to "the good thief," the man
who had been a lifelong reprobate, and was dying as a just
punishment for his crimes. He turns to Jesus, seeking forgiveness; and instantly he is answered with words that ever since
they were spoken have brought comfort and hope to every
penitent sinner: "This day thou shalt be with Me in paradise."
The echoing of another Word in our memory reminds us
that almost with His last breath Jesus gave His Mother to St.
John, and also — as the Church teaches — to us. It is that
bequest which leads us to honor her as her Son did, and leaves
us confident that she will care for us no less tenderly than a
mother for her child.

With the cry, "I thirst," our Lord revealed the anguish which
would inevitably result from a savage scourging followed by
crucifixion; and the echo of that cry is like a new revelation
of the length to which God's children must sometimes go if
they are to be completely obedient to the will of the heavenly
Father. Our sense of the agony undergone by Jesus is deepened
as we recall His words: "Father, why hast Thou forsaken Me?"
Then, with His mission completed, even to the last detail, He
says: "It is finished." And to His Father: "Into Thy hands I

commend My spirit." Having thus spoken, He died. We are stirred with the almost irresistible hope that we shall be able to echo His words; and that when our individual lives come to an end, we, too, shall be able to say, "I have done what the heavenly Father called me to do."

As narrated by the Evangelists, the disciples, with Pilate's permission, wrapped the Lord's Body in a winding sheet and laid it in a tomb. A winding sheet still preserved at Turin is, in the judgment of a considerable number of experts, the identical linen cloth in which the Body was wrapped. They base their opinion upon the age of this linen cloth; the burial customs common among the Jews at the time of the Crucifixion; the known effect which aromatic mixtures combined with sweat and blood would have made upon this type of cloth. Actually the stains upon the Turin relic do form a negative from which positive photographs have been made. These, when looked at carefully, convey to many the sense of having an actual photograph of what happened on Calvary nineteen centuries ago. To be sure, the moving experience does not change our previous knowledge of the story of the Passion; but it does arouse a new and possibly more lasting sense of the reality of what occurred at that distant date. The event has been not merely described in human records, but physically registered in a material way, discernible to human sense.

What then? Only that henceforward we should be better able to remember, to realize, to respond to what happened on that day long passed when One, who had been born as a human infant for our sakes, shed His blood and died for us in order that we, instead of remaining helpless and despairing sinners, might be lifted forever beyond the reach of evil, and by the power of His never ending grace transformed into holy men and women, fit to enter into heaven.

"MY CHURCH"

O N THIS rock I will build My Church," said our
Lord. He had come from heaven to show men
how to develop the nascent likeness of God in the soul. He
wished His teaching to be passed on to future generations.
Obviously it would be impossible for individual men to go to
Scripture and by private judgment ascertain the correct answers
to the various questions which would ordinarily suggest themselves, as new generations of mankind faced new circumstances
and new problems. Even private wills, even political constitu-
tions and civil laws need courts to interpret them — otherwise
there will inevitably be dissension. In the absence of a divinely
established authority commissioned to speak in our Lord's
name, there would arise as many forms of "Christianity" as
individual opinion might suggest. The history of heresies shows
this to be no idle fancy. Unity of belief has been preserved
only in the Church commissioned to interpret our Lord's teaching. When disputes arise, the Catholic turns to the Church and
asks for a decision. It is a fact of tremendous significance that
the Church, which undertakes to interpret Christ's teaching
infallibly, has discharged this office for many centuries, without
in so doing stultifying or contradicting herself.

The Church's commission to define Christ's teaching is an
echo of His words: "Upon this rock I will build My Church;
and the gates of hell shall not prevail against it." It is the

Church's duty to check the spread of disunity, to forestall the corruption of the authentic tradition. That she alone can do this, makes her unique. To what other teacher can a man go to obtain divinely guaranteed answers to questions about the meaning of the Last Supper, or about Christ's law with regard to marriage? The Church gives a definite answer; and our acceptance of this answer becomes the test of our Catholicity. Outside the Church, by contrast, confusion prevails.

But a question presents itself: Can we identify the Catholic Church of the present day with the Church of apostolic times? To that question, John Henry Newman provided a convincing answer. At a time when he was conspicuous as a leader of the High Church Party in the Church of England, he had been accused of leading that Church Romeward. This charge he denied, affirming that he and his associates were attempting to get rid of the deviations sanctioned by Rome, and to re-establish the apostolic Church. Later, having begun to feel uncertain about his position, he went into retirement to examine it more carefully, and as his studies progressed, he saw to his dismay that there was no essential difference between the apostolic Church of the early centuries and the Church of Rome in the nineteenth century. He published the result of his study in his celebrated *Essay on the Development of Christian Doctrine*. On the last page of it, having made clear his decision to seek admittance into the Catholic Church, he added these touching words.

Such were the thoughts concerning the "Blessed Vision of Peace," of one whose long-continued petition had been that the Most Merciful would not despise the work of His own Hands, nor leave him to himself; — while yet his eyes were dim, and his breast laden, and he could but employ Reason, in the things of Faith. And now, dear Reader, time is short, eternity is long. Put not from you what you have here found; regard it not as mere matter of present controversy; set not out resolved to refute it, and looking about for the best way of doing so; seduce not yourself with the imagination that it comes of disappointment, or disgust, or restlessness, or wounded feeling, or undue sensibility, or other weakness. Wrap not yourself round in the associations of years past; nor determine that to be truth which you wish to be so, nor make an idol of cherished anticipations. Time is short. Eternity is long.

Newman is one of a multitude of scholarly, religious men who have followed along the same road. They have accepted what every Catholic believes; namely, that the Bishop of Rome is the legitimate successor of Peter, to whom Christ said, "Thou art Peter, and upon this rock I will build My Church."

THE PERFECT ANSWER

WE OWE much to St. Peter. Especially are we indebted to him for his reply to our Lord after certain disciples, aghast at Christ's foretelling of the Eucharist, had turned away. Jesus said to the Twelve: "Will you also go away?" Peter made the perfect answer: "Lord, to whom shall we go?"

These words grow more significant the more we reflect upon them. They set us face to face with the alternative that must be accepted if we turn away from Christ. Human history gives compelling evidence of the wisdom of Peter's choice. Do men and women who turn away from our Lord ever remain content? They may speak bold words; they may present smiling faces to the world; but we do not envy them; we feel that nothing would persuade us to follow their example. We find countless proofs that even when fainthearted disciples who renounce their loyalties gather honors and wealth and popularity, rarely are they without tragic regrets. How often they wish that they could roll back the tide of time and have a chance to make their choice all over again! How sharp is the contrast between them and those faithful Christians who follow their Lord to the end with reverence and confidence! These die with joy in their hearts even though they are poor or outcasts or martyrs racked and burned. Each one of them gives new testimony to the wisdom of following our Lord.

Not many years ago when the fairly smooth life of one prospective convert seemed about to be disrupted by her conversion to Catholicism, a practical-minded friend of her family warned that painful repercussions were likely to follow. Grief would be brought to other members of her family; religious division would replace the old harmony. And the friend wound up with the challenging climax: "There must be some less devastating way than this of getting whatever it is you want." But another friend, to whom that affirmation seemed "little short of blasphemy," pointed to a crucifix and said, "Must there have been a less devastating way than that?"

After all, the cross is the *symbol* of our religion. When you were admitted to membership in the Catholic Church by baptism, did not the priest, as if by warning, say, "Receive the sign of the cross on forehead and on heart." There was a fair warning that to be a Christian one must be ready to carry any cross laid upon one's shoulders by the hand of God. The cross marks our sure path to heaven.

The Imitation of Christ puts all this very strongly and clearly in that memorable chapter which closes Book II: "The sign of the cross will be in heaven when the Lord shall come to judge. Then all the servants of the cross, who in their lifetime have conformed themselves to the Crucified, shall come to Christ their judge with great confidence. Why then art thou afraid to take up thy cross which leads to a kingdom?"

Peter's perfect answer may well ring in our ears, when we are tempted to leave the path of duty for what promises to be a more pleasant, or profitable, or socially attractive road with a happy ending. No such promise can possibly be true; for no such road exists. This does not mean that the true disciple must turn away from every human joy, from every sunlit path, from every pursuit that brings temporal honor or profit. But it does mean that when an issue confronts us, we must never turn away from Jesus. In the days of the early martyrs, a judge would often ask a Christian merely to place a pinch of incense in the brazier before the statue of an idol, in order thus to signify his renunciation of Christ. The refusal to comply caused countless men and women to be racked and burned and beheaded or thrown into the arena with wild beasts or tied in sacks and cast into the sea. These were the men and women now in heaven whose sufferings are still remembered here on earth by us to whom their faith and constancy give the light and courage we need. Many of them we know by name; countless others remain nameless. But their heroic story in the Roman martyrology is read daily in practically every Catholic religious community. These martyred saints, known and unknown, are your fathers and mothers and sisters and brothers. You belong to their family. If ever you are asked to turn away from Christ, reply as they replied, with the answer that Peter made, *The Perfect Answer*.

To be sure, my testing may not deal with martyrdom, or the leaving of family and friends to enter the religious life. It may be concerned with such ordinary things as attendance at daily Mass or frequent reception of Holy Communion or an austere daily routine or the practice of works of zeal and charity among poor, sick, irreligious persons. Whatever the issue be, it should receive always the same answer. For to turn my back on Christ is unutterably foolish, unthinkably disloyal. The road of duty sometimes may be so rough that, even though we see the outlines of our Lord's figure ahead, and hear His invitation to follow, we begin to consider the possibility of discovering some other smoother road. Then Peter's words re-echo in our consciousness; and we say to ourselves, "To whom shall we go?" The wildly absurd alternative presents itself: WE SHALL HAVE TO FIND A BETTER LEADER THAN JESUS CHRIST.

THE MYSTICAL BODY

IT IS not encyclopedic records nor scientific laboratories nor the psychologist's probings that help men most effectively in their search for wisdom. They are aided far more by revelation. The Old Testament tells of man's creation, of his first sin, of his punishment. The New Testament describes the coming of the Redeemer, His dying upon the cross, His founding of the Church to preserve and interpret His revelation, answer men's greatest problems, point out the road that leads to endless peace.

Catholics, looking back at the Church's long history, are excusably proud. We find comfort in the great impression which the Church makes upon the world, in the tributes given to her enduring majesty and her unique influence. We dwell happily upon Macaulay's stirring tribute to the Church which reminds everyone that the line of supreme pontiffs, running back to the days before the Saxon had set foot in Britain or the Frank had crossed the Rhine, "makes the proudest noble houses seem like newcomers."

This gratifying appraisal should not, however, withdraw our attention from the immeasurably truer conception of the Church presented by Pius XII. He points out that the greatness of our religion depends not on size or age or prestige; that the Church is properly defined as the Mystical Body of Christ;

68

that the characteristic privilege of her children is to share the Christ-life, and to be united with our Lord and with one another in adoring the heavenly Father, in denying self, in serving mankind. The papal encyclical on the Mystical Body of Christ, describing what lies behind external growth and activity, tells us that the success of missionary activities depends on prayer; and that when individual Catholics live in close union with the Indwelling Spirit this will provide a divine effect in each and every one of them. Our common vocation transcends all differences of race, rank, ability; it embraces priests, laymen, contemplatives, missionaries. Cloistered religious play an important part on the mission front; persons outside convent walls practice contemplative prayer. This is why we may so often look at a great congregation, and, in a spirit like that of the poet, Gray, feel sure not of "some village Hampden," but of many a saint, known to God alone, hidden there.

Commenting on the growth of the missions, Pius XII described the new development of a highly organized world-wide system initiated by Pius XI, promoted by Benedict XV, rounded out by himself; and he summed up by stating that the missionary movement "had gained such force and momentum and attained such proportions as were never before witnessed in the annals of Christian history." Concurrently with that expansion of the missions came further development in the field of prayer. The coincidence should not surprise us; two different fires blaze brightly when both are fanned by the same wind. We do not expect to find a prayerful soul empty of zeal, nor to come upon a zealous apostle who never prays. We do anticipate that if the stream of prayer dwindles, apostolic zeal will dry up.

It is enlightening to recall that, after the excesses of the Quietists in the seventeenth century had aroused prejudice against the Catholic tradition of contemplative prayer, missionary activities soon sank to a very low level. By the nineteenth century many of the faithful had come to look upon "social service" as the real test of the good life. Omens of spiritual reawakening however, appeared with the publication of Cardinal Manning's two books on the Holy Ghost, and the re-editing of famous old works by the Benedictines, Augustine Baker and Blosius, the Jesuits, Caussade and Lallemant, and others. Especially important for the revival of the contemplative ideal was Pope Leo's encyclical on the Holy Ghost published in 1897. Possibly Pope Leo shared Cardinal Manning's opinion that Protestantism had swept like wildfire through Europe in the sixteenth century because the Catholic people were unaware of the doctrine of the Indwelling of the Holy Ghost in the soul. At any rate Pope Leo's encyclical aroused the world to a new realization of that teaching; and the years that followed gave evidence of this reawakening, both in the publication of precious old books, and in the appearance of new works emphasizing the value of the simple type of prayer inspired by devotion to the Holy Spirit.

Soon after the appearance of the encyclical on the Holy Ghost came the *Autobiography* of the young Carmelite, later canonized, St. Teresa of Lisieux. Multitudes were attracted by her practice of childlike prayer and her apostolic zeal. The faithful manifested new interest in the cloister; many monasteries arose; the Maryknoll missionaries and other communities developed groups of cloistered contemplatives. Despite the appalling spread of crime and the long wars, devotion to the Sacred Heart and to the Rosary of the Blessed Virgin grew steadily.

Early in the twentieth century, *The Soul of the Apostolate,* written by Dom Chautard, a Trappist monk, became "the bedside book" of Pope Pius X. As if by prophetic instinct, the Holy Father began to prepare his flock for an approaching era in which the hierarchy was to be increasingly dependent upon the co-operation of the laity; the era in which the younger generation would assume new independence and new importance; the era which would be dominated so largely by "the common man."

Two papal decrees on Holy Communion, revolutionizing the practice previously current, declared daily Communion to be not the privilege of a select few, but the right of every Catholic properly disposed; and the Pope set the age for First Communion at the dawn of reason. The startled older generation looked on with amazement while little children, six or seven years old, approached the altar rail; while multitudes of working men and women received Holy Communion before going to their daily work or, in some cases, at the noon hour; while youngsters at a dance would watch the clock as midnight approached, so that they might be sure to remain fasting for Communion the next morning. Then came later legislation further mitigating the rules of the eucharistic fast in various ways including permission to drink water at any time; and, in 1957, a decree authorized the reception of Holy Communion after three hours' fast from solid food and one hour fast from liquids.

Results have brought emphatic justification of the new discipline. A large proportion of surprisingly confident young persons developed into priests and nuns and missionaries, or into parents who taught holiness to their children, or into lay apostles devoted to every conceivable kind of charitable and religious work. Their achievements are recalled by the mere mention of Catholic Action; the Lay Apostolate; the Students' Mission Crusade; the Retreat Movement; the Liturgical Movement; Third Orders; The Legion of Mary. The Lay Associates of one community numbered nearly 100,000.

If it is significant that, early in the present century, an outstanding volume on the apostolate of the laity came from a Trappist monk, it seems no less significant that fifty years later the Carthusian, Dom Moore, urged the laity to participate in the apostolate by means of contemplative prayer. This veteran psychologist, in his book, *The Life of Man with God*, supplemented general instruction on the spiritual life with information gathered personally from case histories and from a widely distributed questionnaire.

The first part of his book sets forth facts which bear upon the development of an unselfish, prayerful, apostolic mode of life. Addressing himself to the "little people" who aspire to closer union with God, the author describes a number of typical individuals plodding along the path that leads to contemplative prayer and heroic virtue; a young priest in a parish; a Sister in a hospital; a missionary in China; a nun at the head of a science department; a woman physician; a steamfitter; a crippled little girl. One paragraph reminds us that the apostolate of prayer and self-denial is open to those for whom all other gates are closed: "the hopeless invalid, the blind, the cripple, the poor, the ignorant; for all these can love God and offer sacrifice to Him." Here, then, an experienced educator, an expert in the field of psychiatry, who professes and practices monastic ideals, is encouraging the laity to aspire to contemplative prayer; and he cites unimpeachable authorities to justify his teaching. This should help to dissipate the uncertainty of persons who respect Americans for their success in organizing, staffing, and supporting missions, but still seem dubious about their adaptability to the practice of contemplation.

It has never been a simple task for the Church to fulfill her divine commission. She has had to face the opposition not only of the weakling and the sensualist, but also of the physically and intellectually powerful. Yet for nearly twenty centuries she has preserved Christ's teaching without distortion. The persons who live up to her laws and precepts and admonitions, the graduates of her spiritual school, the saintly men and women whom she recognizes as her best children are outstanding among history's heroic figures. Her *Schola Sanctorum* contains a countless multitude, from every class and type, every age and every land, who under her guidance have reflected the ideals Jesus presented as His own.

The central aim of the Church's teaching and legislating is to establish and solidify the proper relationship between the soul and its Maker. She insists that the laws of the kingdom of God bind not less strictly, but more strictly, than the laws of nature. The divine edicts oblige us to control mind and will so that our imaginary independence will be replaced by wholehearted adoration, and our pleasure-seeking will give way to the acceptance, sometimes even to the choosing, of pain. The Church must help man to solve the enigma presented by his double nature — a spiritual soul in an animal body. She must show this dual creature how to become Godlike; for thus and only thus will he be fit for heaven.

FACING THE FACTS

THE Church is essentially realistic. She accepts every proven fact of human experience and every demonstrated truth; she shows how they fit into the plan of the universe which she presents to her children as part of the Faith. Hence every true Catholic must be a realist. This does not mean that we can solve every puzzle or give a definite answer to every mystery; but we are able to show that our Faith is compatible with every proven fact. It is indeed no slight support to the Church's claim of infallibility that, during twenty centuries of existence, she has never imposed on her children, as part of the Faith, anything which then, or later, was demonstrated to be false. Mysteries and problems remain mysteries and problems; but they do not compel reasonable, honest men to repudiate Catholicism.

However, the Church's children breathe the atmosphere which pervades the time and place in which they live; and, therefore, with the good oxygen they inhale much poisonous air. Their neighbors, school companions, friends, associates, teachers are often infected with erroneous theories that deny the existence of God, the divinity of Christ, the authority of the Church. The world around them may hold a pseudo philosophy which depreciates, or wholly denies, the moral law, the need of social and religious authority, the validity of a religion which undertakes to inculcate a sense of sin, the need of repentance, the necessity of internal and external acceptance of an existing articulate divine authority. And situations often arise in which individual Catholics must accept the Church's guidance and obey her instructions even in matters that lie outside the field of her infallibility. For the Church, in the discharge of the office imposed on her by Christ, is obliged to guard the moral and doctrinal health of her children even more carefully than natural parents guard the physical life of their little ones. In so doing she issues directions and, to these, good Catholics should conform wholeheartedly so that even outside the field of infallible teaching they will "think with the Church." In the long run, this procedure will not really narrow their outlook but safeguard them from error.

From time to time, then, we should undertake a reappraisal of our attitude toward some of the more conspicuous and dangerous misconceptions which prevail in our generation. Among these is the notion that the Church requires the surrender of all individual freedom and looks with suspicion on any display of personal initiative. This action may lead an outsider to look with aversion on Catholics because "they seem to be content with following and obeying, never think or act for themselves, merely wait to be told by the Church, or by a priest, what to do and how to do it."

This is a gross misunderstanding. Authority no more destroys the proper function of the private judgment than it destroys the function of the private conscience. Its office is to guide and assist both judgment and conscience, and then leave them to tread the path and bear the burden themselves. To say that reason alone is inadequate, does not mean that it is to be set aside altogether; neither does the fact that faith is built upon revelation imply that every inference and every deduction is infallibly true; that all our customs and all our institutions are divinely established or that every instructor of whatever rank speaks with the same finality. "Are all apostles? Are all prophets? Are all doctors?" We observe a certain discrimination and retain a certain sense of proportion. Within reason's own realm, where it is ruler and judge, we pay all due respect to argument; we listen heedfully to the suggestions of common sense. To refuse to open our minds to the light, to overlook any little seed of evidence, would hardly help to make us good and faithful servants of truth.

A Protestant, who had become interested in the Church, once made a priest almost speechless by asking, "If I should become a Catholic, would I have to give up my present habit of kneeling down and using my own words to ask God to help me when I am in trouble?" How could he ever have absorbed such an idea! Perhaps because Catholics sometimes seem to exaggerate outer forms to an absurd degree — as if they were not at liberty to deal with God simply, as if they could not make a good confession until they had memorized the Act of Contrition printed in a prayer book. They sometimes become victims of their own strength — like "muscle-bound" persons whose tissues are too large and tense to be properly elastic. We are so richly provided with spiritual helps — so wisely directed by the Church's precise formulation of divine truth and her bestowal of specific sacramental graces — that we may forget these precious things are intended to aid each individual soul toward inner personal union with God in mind and will. The Church does not impose on us the unintelligent repetition of formulas, nor the substitution of lip service for interior acceptance. The Catholic ideal is to aim at personal, intimate, supremely real union with the Creator. This union is to be developed in each one of us through co-operation with God's gifts of grace. Religious life that consists only of words and external acts is counterfeit. If made up chiefly of these elements, it is weak and shaky.

By way of contrast, certain professed "Christians," confident of finding the way to heaven without help from any person or any institution, are bold enough to say, "I don't need a church!" This may sound good to some, because "independence" and "self-reliance" are sacred words in our American tradition. Yet self-reliance, when distorted, can take on a meaning at least implicitly immoral. Only those who prize that type of independence will conclude that Catholics are necessarily out of tune with American self-reliance. The roots of this myth reach back to the private-judgment theory which rejected the Christian tradition of sixteen centuries. Its fruit is the education which trains men in the fatal doctrine that each individual is, and should be, independent of everyone else. But all sane persons recognize definite limits to independence. In what sense would a man be "independent" if he were on a little rock ten feet square in mid-Pacific? An old tale tells that Caesar absurdly assured his boatman that no storm could wreck the craft in which Caesar was passenger. We betray an egotism no less absurd when we dare to think that we are completely self-reliant.

Another departure from sound sense is the theory of "secularism" which holds that man can get along well without any supernatural religion whatever. I may in a limited sense declare, "I am the captain of my soul," without being so foolish as to mean that I need no rudder, no chart. For, each one of us does ultimately determine his own spiritual fate by accepting or rejecting the opportunity offered him by God. But, as every sane person must admit, there are countless achievements utterly beyond the power of any one man, or of all the men in the world working harmoniously to the limit of their natural abilities. Much harm is done by administering "tranquilizers" to conscience. The propagandist of some new cult may persuade you to believe that the world is yours for the taking; but when the fever of enthusiasm abates, you realize how helpless you would be if you, unarmed, were confined in a cell with a raging tiger.

Some of the secularist foolishness seems to affect certain Catholics at times — for example, those who, imagining that they can get along quite well without the aid of sacramental grace, therefore neglect frequent Communion or go into near occasions of sin boldly. Persons of this type resemble the rash man who had to be restrained by the police from trying to swim the Niagara River, just above the Falls; or the reckless souls who "play with fire"; or the even more reckless type who feel confident that they may safely sin and then later repent.

An offshoot of secularism is a theory of education which divides Catholics from many of their fellow citizens. The position of the Church on education is clear to all the world. She regards religious education as one of the inalienable rights of the child. Parents must be ready to make every reasonable sacrifice of their resources in order to protect that right. The steps to be taken in providing the proper education will, of course, vary with circumstances; but the obligation to respect the child's right to a fitting education always rests upon the parents' conscience. And on the whole, the watching world — even when unsympathetic with the Church's dogmatic teaching — admires the heroic efforts made by Catholic parents to ensure that their children receive their rightful religious training.

In sober truth, persons properly responsive to the Church's teaching are the world's true realists. Although they cannot explain mysteries, at least they know how to deal with them. They face the universe with all its actualities and all its possibilities — joys and sorrow, fact and fable, time and eternity, wealth and poverty, sin and holiness. They mirror God's will in their own; and they can go straight to the mark in the darkest night, in the cruelest pain.

OUR LADY

I T SEEMS almost like a sour note in a lovely song,
when persons who profess to love our Lord speak
rudely about His Blessed Mother. Father Faber argues against
them thus:

> But scornful men have coldly said
> Thy love was leading me from God;
> And yet in this I did but tread
> The very path which Jesus trod.

Early in life the well-trained Catholic acquires a habit of
reverential affection for our Lady; and, despite all differences
between race and race, family and family, person and person,
this reverence has been an outstanding feature of the Catholic
character down through the centuries. The same attitude toward
Mary which was characteristic of her divine Son has become
a recognized characteristic of the Catholic. Little wonder, then,
that a Catholic child is puzzled when widening experience
brings him in contact with other Christian children who do not
act toward the Blessed Virgin as he has been taught to do.
"How can this be?" he asks. And well he might! Was there
anything improper or unholy or unworthy of imitation in our
Lord's conduct? Is it possible that He acted toward His mother
as little Protestant children are taught to act? Was He suspicious of her or distrustful? Surely not! The fact is that in His

relationship with His Mother, Jesus must always have acted at
least as affectionately as the typical Catholic child.

It seems only fair, however, to add to our criticism of the
attitude of some Protestants an acknowledgment that others
gladly recognize our Lady's claim to a supreme position among
creatures — Wordsworth, for example, who wrote:

> Mother whose virgin bosom was uncrossed
> By any shade of thought to sin allied,
> Woman above all women glorified,
> Our tainted nature's solitary boast.

Anyone who studies the nature of heresies carefully will
appreciate the significance of Newman's comment — that those
groups which departed from the Catholic tradition with regard
to the Blessed Virgin eventually lost faith in the divinity of
our Lord. It seems an inevitable process of deterioration. One
who fears that a tribute to God's most perfect creature might
detract from the honor due to God Himself seems already
unaware of the infinite distance that separates the human from
the divine, the creature from the Creator. The care with which
the Church guards against any misconception of this sort is
illustrated in the Litany of the Saints, so impressively chanted
on various liturgical occasions. Addressing God first, and rising
to a climax with "Holy Trinity, One God, *have mercy* on us,"
the litany then, as it moves down an infinite distance to the
level of the greatest of all creatures, chants the appeal, "Holy
Mary, *pray* for us."

A correct notion of the divinity of Christ excludes the possibility that honor given to the Blessed Mother may be confused
with the honor due her Son. Moreover, the Church is here not
only teaching sound doctrine, but also providing a solid basis
for devotion; and impartial observers have been quick to see
that the Catholic attitude toward the Blessed Mother is of

enormous practical value in making Christians more childlike and more pure.

Wordsworth has already been mentioned as one of the many outsiders who share the Catholic belief that our Blessed Lady is entitled to a reverence altogether unique. We find examples of this reverential spirit also in the verses of the Protestant poet, Longfellow. He compares Catholic prayers for Mary's intercession to the appeal made by little children who, after having offended their father, are rather ashamed to approach him directly. Therefore they

> Speak with their sister, and confiding, wait
> Till she goes in before and intercedes.

The display of reverence by means of spoken words and physical gestures and material symbols, traditional in the Church, accords perfectly with universal human custom in all types of relationships. But words and actions, if sincere, are manifestations of an interior attitude; and Catholic devotion to the Blessed Mother is essentially interior. Here, as in all vocal prayer, our chief reason for using words is that they aid us in one way or another. We must, of course, exercise proper vigilance to keep ourselves from dropping into exaggeration and insincerity — a fault easy enough for the average human being to commit. But when prayer degenerates into a merely external act, it is a pose, a sham. It becomes something meaningless; it justifies the Protestant suspicion. Let us not forget that a very short prayer, uttered only within the soul, is better than fifteen, or fifty, decades recited without any internal accompaniment.

It must not be imagined that the high honor we pay to our Blessed Lady is a modern novelty, unknown in the early Church. The doctrine of the Incarnation involved the Catholic teaching and the Catholic practice with regard to our Lady, although some of the implications were only gradually perceived; and we may be confident that the attitude toward the Blessed Virgin which Catholics are now trained to take is essentially in harmony with the apostolic Church.

This does not deny the possibility of sentimentalism and extravagance, both of which may easily creep into a devotion radically sound. Danger lies at both extremes. There can be too much emotion or there can be too little; and if the latter fault is less conspicuous it may, nevertheless, be more dangerous. Not by mere chance is a high degree of fervor toward our Lady related to the possession of true sanctity and also to the cultivation of true devotion in a household or, indeed, in a country or a generation. One would deserve to be classed as cynical if one were never stirred by a sense of being in contact with true prayer when the *Ave Maria* is sung by an artist both gifted and devout. And it would be almost less than human to deny the quality of prayer to the *Salva Regina* when Trappists chant that favorite hymn of theirs at the end of the night Office in the monastery.

III.

SEVEN DEVILS

IT IS not, indeed, correct to describe the seven Capital Sins as seven devils; but the two groups have in common at least this — both represent the deformity, the perversion, of what originally was good.

The Capital Sins are not sins in the ordinary sense of the word. They are inclinations; but, again, not in the usual meaning. For they are not acquired by the individual, but inherited; and strengthened or weakened, by that individual's conduct. They are innate proclivities — each one of them rooted in a useful tendency which inclines a person to seek a definite natural good. It is when they are overdeveloped, so to say, that they become disorderly and run counter to the soul's best interests. As forces for evil, they are so powerful that they seem to be, and are frequently called, "diabolic." Thus in common usage the word "passion" suggests an intense emotional drive which beats down reason and free will, and provides at least a partial excuse for misdeeds.

On the other hand, an unabridged dictionary shows that the word "passion" has an amazing number of alternate meanings; it is not to be classified as good or evil without further investigation. The Liturgy speaks of the "Passion of Christ." We think of the "passionate" weeping of a brokenhearted mother as akin to "holy." There is such a thing as "passionate" devotion to liberty and justice. There is also the "passionate" affection of two worldlings which may be sinful.

Theology recognizes passion as a uniquely strong desire, rooted in nature for the purpose of spurring an individual to pursue nature's aims, and so deeply rooted that, when balked, it may render the individual unreasonable and even irresponsible. Largely on this account, the name "Capital Sins" is given to certain habits which often urge the individual toward gratification, regardless of any prohibition set up by God. Conspicuous in our moral life and frequently playing a major role, they well deserve to be classified as "capital."

The Book of Genesis tells that after God had placed our first parents in the Garden of Eden, He commanded them to abstain from eating the fruit of a certain tree; and their disobedience resulted in their fall from grace. The common theological teaching is that their offense was caused by pride — that God's friendship was lost because man chose to regard himself as center of the universe; because he let himself be dominated by egotism; because he preferred his own will to the will of God.

As today we observe the conflicts that disturb and destroy individual souls, we are impressed by the theory that the primal transgression which crippled man's nature, the offense which "brought sin into the world and all our woe," was indeed the sin of pride. Absurdly, the head of the human race thrust God aside and, for the moment, had his own way. This was madness. No sane being could imagine that it would be possible to get something worthwhile in spite of God.

The point comes out clearly in the story of Eve's fall. To the question of the Tempter, about her motive for abstaining from the fruit of the tree of knowledge, she replied that God had told her the result of eating it would be death. The Tempter's answer equivalently was: "That is a lie. God is trying to deceive you. Don't believe Him; *believe me!* I am telling the truth." Eve believed the Tempter. She ate in defiance of God's prohibition; and the world came crashing down.

Here is the most startling climax in literature, picturing the most disastrous incident of all human history — a creature decides that it will be profitable to believe Satan and to distrust God. But we quickly detect a disturbing similarity between the tragic madness of our first parents and the madness of every other later sinner, including ourselves. There is no one who consciously disobeys God who is not — at least practically — acting on the theory that it is worthwhile to commit this treachery. After reading the story of Eve's fall, and sternly condemning *her* weakness which cost mankind so much, we come to our senses and begin to realize that *we* have done precisely what she did. We, too, have allowed desire to overcome reason; we, too, have plunged ourselves into calamity; and we, too, remain hopelessly ruined, unless God Himself restores the order which we have shattered. So far as our own resources are concerned, the loss is irreparable. To unscramble eggs would be immeasurably easier than to regain lost innocence.

Had I not better do whatever I can to stamp this lesson indelibly on my memory, so that I shall never again overlook the significance of disobeying God? Willful defiance of Him is sin; it is always sin; it is a blow in the face to our Creator; it is insanity. When I sin, I abandon every prospect of attaining happiness, unless God in His gracious goodness comes to lift me up — the same God whom I have insulted and betrayed.

WHAT FOOLS!

F IRST of the Capital Sins, pride is a sort of poisonous root which bears six other sins as its fatal fruit. In plain speech, pride is a basic instinct of nature which urges us to put self always first. If not restrained, it drives a man to the insane extreme of acting as if he were himself the center of the universe. The implication that he is pushing God aside may not be present to his conscience; but this is actually what he does if he follows his own will instead of conforming to the known will of God. "Evil be thou my good!" was Satan's battle cry; and when we surrender to the pressure of pride, we enroll under his banner and fight on his side. Take a closer look at this vice — so like cancer. How powerful it is! How quick to gain control of a man's whole personality! How long lived! How well concealed! Note a man who ordinarily behaves well; then touch his pride and see how suddenly his whole personality seems to change.

No wonder that our Lord, in training His disciples, pointed out the evil of pride. No wonder that He emphasized the need of cultivating the virtue of humility which automatically excludes pride. In sharp contrast with vicious egotism which infects whatever it touches, humility helps to develop a man's noblest qualities. Unfortunately, worldlings commonly look down upon humility; even though they sometimes use the cloak of pseudo humility to cover up a state of mind which is essentially arrogant and egotistic.

Of the sins which stem from pride, three are largely mental — envy, anger, avarice. Like hair-triggered hammers, they go off at the slightest pressure, even pressure caused by momentary delusion. Later, we find that we have been tricked — that the pleasant drink was poison, that the diamonds were nothing but paste, that the cash was counterfeit. Yet we continue to let ourselves be deceived again and again by the Father of Lies.

Grosser and more distasteful to the fastidious person are pride's other three fruits: gluttony, lust, sloth. These, more obviously than the first trio, tend to change man, made in God's image, into the likeness of a beast. They stem from natural appetites for food, drink, sex, physical comfort — whatever can be classified as sensual gratification. Dominantly material and animal, they may keep us on a low, subhuman level. Present in every normal human being, these fundamentally useful appetites easily develop to an inordinate, unrestrained degree. It takes vigilance and strength to keep them from making us resemble beasts; and, unless brought under the control of reason and will, by hard effort and divine grace, they destroy our souls.

In the endeavor to master the vicious tendencies just named, nothing human is more helpful than the kind of prayer which holds us constantly and consciously in the presence of God — that is to say, keeps us in our proper place. I shall succeed if I focus my attention on Him and if I commune with Him frequently about (1) my total dependence on Him; (2) my immeasurable gratitude for His constant gracious affection and care of me; and (3) my desire to share the burden of carrying His cross, by accustoming myself to relinquish what I like and to accept what I do not like. Following this pattern of conduct with fair consistency, I shall prevent the vicious root of pride from sending forth those six strong tentacles which so effectively drag one down to spiritual death.

If we are to set about the checking and conquering of our devil-like passions, we may well begin with an attempt to identify our chief weaknesses by listing those for which we are most often criticized or those which we most frequently have to confess. The next step is to select the one which would be easiest to correct, to relate it to that capital sin from which it seems to spring, and to undertake to eliminate it entirely — with God's help, of course. This undertaking should begin with the making of a written memo of the fault in question and of the precise brief period — a week or a day to begin with — during which we are to keep it under perfect control. Some surprises may result. For one thing, we shall almost immediately perceive that this favorite minor defect is kindred to that particular capital sin for which we think we have a special aversion. A second discovery may well be that a definite resolution can be kept with comparative ease for a very brief period. We are now really on the way to success.

A fundamental requisite for all improvement, then, is to realize that pride, the source of sin, must be checked by humility. If to put self first is the root of all evil, the plain remedy must be to put God first. And if I do not put God first, how can I defend myself against the charge of being literally irrational, incurably foolish?

EGOTISM

I T IS a startling, but also an illuminating, discovery, when we realize that the first sin, which led to every other sin, and very definitely to all *my* sins, stems from the intrusion of self into the place that belongs to God. Pride, like a potent drug, induces spiritual astigmatism; makes me incapable of seeing things in their true proportion; presents to my vision a distorted universe of which I, myself, am center. To call this "astigmatism" is an understatement. We might better say that pride puts me out of touch with reality, and is really the beginning of madness.

I may succeed in deceiving myself for a while, imagining I am really what I would desire to be, that I have qualities which will win for me the esteem of my neighbors. "Wishful thinking" is the name given to this flight from reality. By appropriating imaginary virtues and overlooking actual faults, I come to resemble a person admiring himself in a huge convex mirror. His image takes on such enormous proportions that it fills the entire landscape, leaving nothing else visible. The comparison is hardly overdrawn. For the mental universe of the egotist is crowded with what seems desirable and important to him. It may be that my words and deeds disclose my weaknesses to the observing world; but, on the other hand, it may happen that, by a subtle process of "covering up," I contrive to deceive my neighbors. I lead them to think I am virtuous, while in fact I am posing in order to gain their respect. Mine is "the pride that apes humility, the devil's darling sin." How often in the past have I put myself and my preference in first place, thrusting God and His will into second place, seeing not the universe that God created, but a creation of my own imagination. If I come to grips with reality, I shall soon find that I have betrayed myself by submitting to a treacherous inner tendency which operates independently of my reason and of my will.

An amazing and humiliating illustration of this typical human defect is offered by the phenomenon called "projected egotism" — a habit so irrational that only reluctantly do I admit its existence in myself. Having thrown the mantle of my projected ego over everything with which I am or have been, even remotely, associated, I become sensitive to any criticism directed toward whatever may seem to be connected with myself — any person, place, race, country, town, street, that was ever in any sense "mine." Take, for example, my emotional disturbance over a fancied slur. Suppose someone laughingly reports that by a curious coincidence he has met, on six successive days, six different persons whose names begin with the letter B; and each of them was a bore. Now, if my name happens to be "Bernard," an emotional disturbance occurs within me, I am annoyed; perhaps I blush or scowl or make an unpleasant remark. But if my name happens to be "Sam," I merely laugh. How silly can I be? The answer is — there is no limit to the silliness of a person under the influence of egotism.

It would, however, not be true to call the projection of one's ego always irrational or despicable. At times it is a virtue, and even an obligation. Duty bids me show special care and affection toward all persons bound to me by special ties, imposed on me by the laws of nature or voluntarily assumed.

It would be wrong to ignore the validity of the claims upon me made by parent or child or neighbor or Church or country. To remain shut up within the confines of self would be wicked perversity. Anyone oblivious of this reversal of "projected egotism" falls under the censure of the Fourth Commandment of the Decalogue, and of the teaching of the Gospel. Here again, however, as always, one must refrain from excess. What would otherwise be a duty is canceled out if it conflicts with justice and upsets good order. "He that loves father or mother more than Me, is not worthy of Me," said our Lord. For activity on each lower level has to be harmonized with order on each higher level, all the way up to the order established by the will of God.

If I reflect on these things, I may well discover within myself certain hitherto unnoticed trends which move me unconsciously to substitute my own will for God's will, and to magnify my own reputation at the expense of His honor and glory. Looking around more sharply and methodically than before, I may begin to see certain good opportunities passed by and certain fine impulses not yet obeyed. Perhaps I have often ignored chances to serve those who, in Christ's teaching, come under the classi-fication of "neighbor" — the poor, the sick, the prisoner, the spiritually destitute. Did I ignore them because they are not *my* neighbors, because they do not "belong to my set"? Perhaps in planning my activities for a day or a week, and in budgeting my expenditures, I give no thought to the paying of my "debts" to the helpless, the depressed, the submerged. What about the poet's challenge? "Is there no beggar at your gate?" Have I not been indifferent to many an appeal, written or spoken, that stressed the desperate need for recruits to fill the thin ranks of those volunteers who work in the field of charity and religion? History records the appalling sufferings undergone by millions of human beings whose rights and privileges have been trodden underfoot by roughshod anger, envy, avarice, gluttony, sloth. Egotistical man has changed the world created by God into a depressing world. How clearly I see now that because egotism is opposed to the will of God, it *must* be destructive of order; and because it destroys order, it must be a perennial source of evil. And meanwhile our Lord's teaching shows me that true charity — the antithesis of egotism — will not only make me resemble God, but will contribute to the healing of the wounds that torment mankind.

FOUR SQUARE

CHARACTER is an indefinite sort of word that clamors for a descriptive adjective. We ask, is it a good or a bad, a straightforward or a sinister, character? Is it strong or weak, magnificent or despicable, childlike or tricky, admirable or repulsive, saintly or base, thrifty or extravagant, Christian or pagan, and so on. We say, "I thought that woman was a weak character, but she showed herself to be a real heroine!" or "This man seemed to be a strong character, yet he went to pieces in a crisis!" Then there is such a thing as a "sacramental character," stamped on the soul at Baptism, Confirmation, and Holy Orders so indelibly that it can never be effaced. For the moment let us concern ourselves with the meaning of the phrase "building character," which obviously must refer to a character not yet hardened into a particular pattern.

St. Thomas, like every sane thinker, holds that a man who sets out to build should know what he is trying to build. If a parent were to say to a teacher, "Look carefully after the development of my child's character," the teacher might very well inquire, "What kind of character?" Presumably it should fit the child for the future — but for what type of future? social? commercial? spiritual? For the present life or for eternity? That reply makes sense. Before we set out to build a character, we have to decide what type of character is most desirable, and what means are necessary for its development. To state this obvious truth seems superfluous, almost ridiculous. Yet, if in a group of persons representative of the contemporary world, each were asked to state specifically what kind of character is most desirable, endless argument would follow — because there would be no unanimity as to the final aim.

It is but rational — it is also extremely important — that each of us should build the sort of character which will aid us to gain everlasting peace. Therefore, we should turn for guidance to our Lord, who undertook to point out the perfect way of life and who gave us the Church to preserve and interpret His teaching for all men and all times.

The Christian concept of character may be likened to a solid, four-square structure, supported at each corner by one of the virtues called "cardinal" — from the Latin word *cardo* (hinge). These virtues — Justice, Prudence, Fortitude, Temperance — looked at collectively, are seen to be features, or ramifications, of that divine order which reflects God's own will. Looked at individually, justice, most comprehensive of the four, seems to be — and often is so described in Holy Scripture — the equivalent of "righteousness." It implies the fulfillment of every obligation. The old adage, *Suum cuique* (To each his own), puts it all in a nutshell, reminding us of the rule of life that our Lord gave to a questioner, "Render to Caesar the things that are Caesar's; and to God the things that are God's." A complete rule of life, indeed! For if I give God His due, I shall be just; I shall withhold from no man what belongs to him. And if I am a just man, I shall by implication be prudent, courageous, and temperate too. Incidentally, we may remind ourselves that justice is concerned not only with material things, but also with less tangible matters as, for example, reputation, peace of mind, spiritual opportunities. It would be unjust to injure our neighbor in any of these respects.

The virtue of prudence demands conformity to the requirements of order; it dictates the doing of the right thing, in the right way, at the right time. Today it restrains us; tomorrow it spurs us on. Always it implies enough deliberation — but no more. It involves honest, intelligent decision, followed by exact and firm execution of whatever has been decided upon. A prudent man in every instance selects the best available means for reaching his immediate end, making sure that this means is in harmony with the *ultimate end*. He co-ordinates mental, emotional, volitional activities; and he will also inevitably be just and temperate and courageous.

There seems to remain hardly any particular place for the second two virtues; but there is really much room for fortitude and temperance. Experience teaches that beginnings are comparatively easy; but as we proceed, our initial supply of energy gives out — not only in the physical order, but in the moral as well. We may be strong enough to protest against wickedness in high places; but when reprisals come and no one supports us, real fortitude is required if we are to continue our protest. The courage of the martyrs is stamped indelibly on the memory of mankind because in their conduct the virtue of fortitude stood out conspicuous. Differing from one another in many respects, but identical in their constancy under torment, they remain everlasting symbols of fortitude. The Church's care to keep their memory alive has helped to make fortitude understood, and in some measure practiced, down through the centuries; and this helps us to realize that fortitude will make us spiritual kin of the martyrs.

What now can we say of temperance, except that it reflects the indispensable order which rules the universe from end to end, balancing everything both great and small. Temperance enables us, indeed requires us, to hold the balance between too much and too little, too early and too late, too fast and too slow; it makes us abide by the everlasting valid rule — *Ne-quid nimis*. Without it, no other virtue would exist. For intemperate zeal would drive every virtue to an extreme, thus changing it into a vice. To remain always temperate is an achievement far beyond the ordinary.

The very mention of "intemperate zeal" reminds us of the Church's insistence upon the ideal of temperance in all her training schools. We are warned to beware of intemperance in our practice of mortification, in our cultivation of humility, in our efforts to pray perfectly — briefly, in every field. There is no well-trained novice who has not repeatedly been warned against trying to progress too rapidly. Not infrequently, these warnings are unheeded by otherwise promising souls so spurred on by eagerness and enthusiasm that they too often get out of step and therefore fail to receive the endorsement of the spiritual director or the mistress of novices. One who does not learn to be temperate will in all probability be crippled by overdoing things which of themselves are duties.

A fairly good example is offered by athletes who tell us that a runner's hardest test in foot racing is to hold back at the moment when he can easily pass the man in front. In other words, self-control, an aspect of temperance, is the price of victory. A short-distance runner, when sprinting one hundred yards, is moving nearly twice as fast as a marathon winner who covers fifteen miles. But if the sprinter should try to maintain his speed for even a mile or two, he would drop down totally exhausted. A good lesson for anyone who in a moment of fervor is tempted to make resolutions generous but rash! *Chi va piano, va sano, e va lontano*. A very free translation of this would be, "Make haste slowly."

Kipling's poem "If" outlines the ideal character cherished by good pagans. It calls upon us to "fill each unforgiving minute with sixty seconds' worth of distance run." The Christian ideal is even more exacting. Who that has read Rosalind Murray's indictment will be satisfied to become a good pagan? Here is her summary:

The Good Pagan "pushed the cart over the hill, and over the brow, and told it to stop halfway down. He dethroned God and put Man in His place, and then demanded the hierarchic pattern: 'You shall all play equal parts, you shall all co-operate!' But it did not work, because it could not work; the orchestra could not play with no conductor; who should play what? At what pace should they play? So it began and so it has continued. . . . The Good Pagan has failed; his regime is over; and with him goes, for most of the intellectual governing class in Europe, the value and the amenities of life. The world is relapsing into barbarism; the Good Pagan, the Gentleman cannot survive."

By way of further emphasizing the contrast between the pagan and the Christian ideals and also underlining the inclusiveness of the latter, one may recall the "Divine Office of the Kitchen," in which Cecily Hallack sings so simply of the joy that filled her soul as she conversed with God while busy with the petty details of household work. Here is part of her petition:

Lord of the pots and pipkins, since I have no time to be
A saint by doing lovely things and vigiling with Thee,
By watching in the twilight dawn, and storming heaven's gates,
Make me a saint by getting meals, and washing up the plates!

Accept my roughened hands because I made them so for Thee!
Pretend my dishmop is a bow, which heavenly harmony
Makes on a fiddle frying pan; it is so hard to clean,
And ah, so horrid. Hear, dear Lord, the music that I mean!

Vespers and compline come to pass by washing supper things,
And mostly, I am very tired; and all the heart that sings
About the morning's work, is gone, before me into bed.
Lend me, dear Lord, Thy Tireless Heart, to work in me instead.

Remind me of the things I need, not just to save the stairs,
But so that I may perfectly lay tables into prayers. . . .

This homely teaching helps one to realize the kind of character that the Christian aims to develop. Including all that is
fine and enviable in Kipling's ideal, it also ensures us against
the Good Pagan's Failure. It reminds us that the proper practice
of ordinary household virtues actually embodies those same stu-
pendous deeds which in the home at Nazareth reflected the
beauty and joy and holiness of God's own heavenly kingdom.
Suddenly we discover in them a sort of echo of St. Paul's
words, unfolding the characteristics of love, enumerating the
specific traits which — he assured the Corinthians — would both
realize an ideal here on earth, and ensure its possession for all
eternity. One need only cultivate charity which "is patient,
envieth not, dealeth not perversely, is not puffed up, is not
ambitious, seeketh not her own, is not inclined to anger,
thinketh no evil, beareth all things, believeth all things, hopeth
all things, endureth all things — and never falleth away." And
charity is greater than the ability to speak as angels speak,
greater than prophetic powers, or inexhaustible knowledge, or
alms-giving — greater than the faith which moves mountains,
greater than martyrdom itself.

ARE YOU SANE?

A SENSITIVE person may shrink from answering the above question. For the correct reply is, "No! — if the question concerns *perfect* sanity." Of course, no one is 100 per cent sound, either mentally or physically. Not every shot of the expert marksman hits the bull's-eye. Baseball experts tell us "nobody bats 1000, even for one season." Since normal people face reality; and since a man previously rated normal would lose that rating if he were to become unhappy because he is not 100 per cent sound, we all must reconcile ourselves to our inevitable defect — not so very embarrassing indeed, since we share it with every other "normal" human being. So we should, without becoming hypersensitive, get acquainted with our own limitations and liabilities; we should be content to be "normally sane"; we should face reality bravely.

If we assume that reality includes everything that exists, we see that there must be different planes of reality. A large part of it exists only in the mind: for example, the memory of things that occurred years ago; my expectations, hopes, intentions; my plans to get ahead, to steal, to kill; my passing of unjust mental judgments; my entertaining of rash suspicions; sinful desires which never became anything more — all these are real. And they greatly enlarge the scope of the world with which I have to deal. Regrets, anxieties, disappointments, dislikes are so real that they exercise secret, but serious, influence upon my moods and my activities, even long after they have passed out of my conscious memory. How wise the old Scholastics were in formulating the rule, "Always distinguish!"

Suppose we reduce the various factors that enter into mental and physical soundness to such simple terms as heredity, then environment, then experience, and finally activities — physical, emotional, mental, volitional, and, of course, moral and religious. It would be a large order to make all the comments that could be passed on this brief summary; so we must be content with a few.

To begin with, each human body inherits many individual peculiarities observable in blood and bone and sinew, in muscular and nervous tissue, in various innate tendencies, abilities, and defects. Although we are responsible for none of these, they affect our whole career, making struggle inevitable, making progress sometimes difficult, sometimes easy. They form part of our endowment; and our Lord's parable about the "talents" reminds us that we are expected to do our best with our allotment. But we are never obliged to do more than our best; we do not have to equal someone more highly gifted.

As to environment — our "education" in the large sense of the word — this includes all that is determined by outside forces. We are not responsible for deficiencies resulting from education which is not of our own choosing. But we *are* responsible for deficiencies resulting from education which we ourselves have chosen. In other words, I am responsible for the good, or bad, use I have made of my "talents," and for the various habits which I have acquired by exercising my will on the material offered by life. And these habits affect not only my ability to make wise decisions, but also my mental and physical health. These habits have gone into the building of my present self and contributed to my rating as equal to the average man, or above, or below.

Looking over the situation, I realize that, although I am not perfectly sane, I can be *reasonably* sane if I select a proper aim and use the means necessary to attain it. This implies that because I am wholly dependent upon God, I must aim to conform to His will; and I must adopt a pattern of conduct in keeping with this aim. If I do this, no person and no thing can keep me from succeeding. If I die trying, I die sane — and in the hereafter I shall become perfectly sane. Unless I quit, I cannot fail.

Now as to the obstacles we face in our progress to perfect sanity! Practically all students of mankind point out that serious trouble is caused by the *duality* of our nature. You and I and everyone possess a soul and a body. Hence we are part spirit, part animal; and we must face the disturbing consequence of this "dichotomy" which drives the lower self to follow one pattern of conduct, whereas the higher self follows another. The ensuing conflict often leads to physical, mental, moral disaster. Robert Louis Stevenson impressed the modern imagination with his tale of Dr. Jekyl, the reputable physician, who — first by choice, and eventually despite his will — was transformed into a vicious criminal. À Kempis is one of many old spiritual writers who anticipated moderns in teaching plainly about "split personality." Long before À Kempis, Plato had likened each individual to a charioteer, trying ineffectually to drive a black and a white steed along a straight road, with the white steed veering in one direction, and the black steed in another. It almost seems as if God implants an angelic spirit in an animal body and sets the soul at the impossible task of transforming the beast into a Godlike being. To an English poet laureate, it looked

> As if some lesser God had made the world,
> But had not power to shape it as He would.

Perhaps we shall best bring the situation home to ourselves if we think of a pet shop where little puppies roam together, much as little children do. The resemblance is striking. Both groups are activated by the same impulse: "Seek pleasure; avoid pain." But the child, after having followed this animal pattern of conduct for a few years, finds himself facing a crisis. Reason makes its appearance and attempts — at the beginning, rather feebly — to substitute a "rational" pattern, based on this new principle: "Do good; avoid evil. Seek the highest good obtainable!"

Reason demands that the growing child should stop acting like a little animal; should begin to search for what is best, even though it hurts; and should establish a pattern of conduct which implies the renunciation of whatever is bad, or less than perfectly good, even though it pleases. But the little animal, which has had a flying start, refuses to give up what is pleasant and to accept what is painful. It resists the command of reason; and, if open defiance proves useless, then the little animal goes underground, and acts like the member of a resistance movement in an invaded country, or like a gangster in a metropolitan underworld. Operating secretly, it often gets its way in spite of reason. And while life lasts, the lower self will never wholly surrender!

The validity of the above description is supported by our own personal experience, and also by the testimony of countless observers, many of them extremely wise and also heroic in virtue. We all learn:

> There is so much good in the worst of us,
> And so much bad in the best of us,
> That it doesn't become any of us
> To talk about the rest of us.

So there we are — everybody! You and I are "drafted for the duration of the war." If we are normally sane, we shall take note of extremely important facts which concern our welfare and, on the basis of these, plan our campaign. Looking at life thus realistically, and training ourselves to control those emotional trends which so easily lead to disorder, we shall eliminate much misbehavior and forestall much unhappiness.

A careful study of human conduct will show that emotional impulses are largely secret; they are nonrational; they are lifelong. They are so secret that sometimes, before a man himself knows it, his neighbors have discovered that he is under pressure. He may claim, "I was not angry" — but his friends could ask, "Why then was your voice shaking, and your hand trembling, and your face flushed?" In a case like this, even before consciousness is aroused, before reason has a chance to function, and certainly before the will has been notified, the endocrine glands have poured secretions into the blood stream, impelling the man to undertake activities, perhaps violent activities. Civil courts take account of this situation. They classify a given offense as a crime of passion, less punishable because indeliberate. Even moral theologians admit a lessening of guilt when passion anticipates volition.

There is no need to stress the point that emotional disturbance frequently leads to irrational conduct. When I yield to a feeling of impatience, I often make it harder for myself to get the thing I most desire. For example, if I wish to win a person to my point of view, and I shout at him because his slowness makes me impatient, I shall probably alienate him and fail of my purpose. Or if, while seeking to make a favorable impression, I manifest conceit or jealousy, I put myself at a great disadvantage. Or if desire for physical comfort makes me a slave to appetite, I may invite grievous suffering by developing into an unhappy invalid, an alcoholic, or a drug addict. Most of us can easily illustrate our readiness to obey irrational impulses, whether in early or in later years. There is an old classical epigram:

I see and approve the better things
But I follow the worse.

The list of capital sins indicates several smooth paths along which we cannot afford to let ourselves glide. We must neither ignore, nor underestimate, these seven passions. Keeping a sharp eye on them, we should follow the counsel of St. Ignatius: *Agere contra!* "Do the opposite of what appetite dictates."

Many faults and much unhappiness may come from uncontrolled emotion — even from anger or dislike which is quite, or almost quite, involuntary. One type of irrational conduct originating in thoughtless response to emotional impulse is manifested by persons who love to serve the helpless, yet fail to discriminate between the various causes, or individuals, they try to benefit. They do harm indirectly by encouraging others to beg, to fawn, to loaf, to shirk responsibility. Some softhearted, incorrigible "do-gooders," some starry eyed idealists, even betray their friends, their country, their religion.

However, certain reactions may be due to constitutional defects; and in that case the individual in question is helpless and blameless. A man may develop neurotic tendencies because he is congenitally hypersensitive; or because he was subjected to overrigorous discipline in youth; or because he has been deprived of normal opportunities for self-expression; or even because total absence of proper discipline has conditioned him to resent all restraint. Neurotic symptoms may spring from a long series of failures, or from a shock following a serious accident, or from a thoughtless custom of doing everything in what seems the easiest way. It is worthwhile, therefore, to advert to the value of discipline, whether self-imposed or administered by others; for discipline, at least in some measure, tends to curb and restrain and perhaps eventually eliminate our irrational, emotional reactions. It is costly to let a small fire become a great conflagration instead of stamping it out in its early controllable stages.

What is implied by "stamping it out"? Without undertaking scientific analysis of the situation, we may advert to certain basic considerations sufficient for present purposes. Understanding our own power, we shall be the better able to use it, and the more successful in attaining control of it. So let us recall that engineers master a force which they *cannot* directly control, by using another force which they *can* directly control — employing fire, for example, or a river current or a gas engine. Now, although I cannot directly control the emotional disturbance provoked by an image in my mind, I can to some extent control it indirectly, if I crowd it out by introducing a *different* image, either pleasant or unpleasant, which is distracting. I may choose an image of something naturally, or supernaturally, delightful; or I may think of something wholly secular, yet filled with interest to me — a play, a story, my next new suit, for example. I may mentally compose a poem, or work on a crossword puzzle. The important feature is that the image must be at least harmless, but also interesting. By systematically pursuing this plan, I may keep an undesirable habit from growing stronger and I may even get rid of it entirely. Briefly then, I should train myself to follow a pattern of conduct favorable to the habits that I wish to acquire, frequently reminding myself of advantages which these habits have brought to others, and will probably bring also to me. This will not always be easy; but it is superlatively worthwhile.

So those who aim to cultivate a rational code of conduct should weigh the following counsels:

1. Get acquainted with your egotistic, animal tendencies.

2. Do not underestimate their power; they have overcome stronger and better persons than you.

3. Train yourself so that you will have a number of powerful,

good habits enlisted on your side. A habit, you know, is a disposition to act in a certain definite way; and, although supernatural habits, such as faith, hope, and charity, can be infused into the soul only by God, natural habits may be acquired by continued free acts of the will.

4. Never lose sight of the profound truth that God's grace will help you to gain many a victory which you could not possibly win unassisted.

Perhaps special attention should be given to the difficulties which come from immaturity. Most of us know that "men are but children of a larger growth." Yet we are still annoyed when told that our own behavior illustrates this same adage — that we ourselves often act like children. It would be good to find out if the criticism is justified; and we may begin by looking at some typical "adolescent characteristics."

Adolescents, in the process of passing from one physical and mental phase to another, undergo a modification of the entire system. At the very time they are experiencing these changes, they also have to readjust their relationships with the outer world of people and things. The double readjustment — subjective and objective, inside and outside — reminds us of a traveler on a fast-moving plane, or train, who has to observe and report on buildings and groups passed en route. His report may well prove to be so unintelligible that he will be required to retrace his route and make a new report. But he has a good excuse; because he had to make so many swift readjustments; about many things he was strongly inclined to say, "Maybe yes," and equally inclined to say, "Maybe no." That same excuse applies also to adolescents whose universe is changing so quickly that they are utterly unable to reconcile the conflict between their inner impulses and the demands made upon them from outside. We must not then, too quickly or too often, find fault with the childishness of a youngster in the early teens. The best we can do is to wait a little while, and then try to give aid by means of a few kindly words.

In the process of developing from adolescence to maturity, the young person needs guidance. Guides may prove to be unskillful; but that chance must be taken by every newcomer in an unknown terrain. In any event, the habit of responding to guidance rather than emotion will establish a certain degree of self-control and develop a certain hesitation about obeying every chance impulse immediately. Fortunate is the youth whose guidance comes from a wise parent, teacher, or friend. Each day and each hour will bring experiences which form a basis for later independent judgment — a judgment which may well be even better than that of the guide, or teacher, who pointed out the first steps.

The suggestions made above may help some persons to pass smoothly from a less mature to a more mature phase of behavior. Sometimes, however, an extremely "immature" type may have to resort to a psychiatrist who perhaps will offer "shock treatment." Even if that treatment does effect a cure, the patient will still be less fortunate than those others who, by making the best possible use of their God-given faculties, by responding to wise teaching, and by praying, have grown out of their immaturity.

Neurologists, like all doctors, take note of symptoms which indicate a patient's susceptibility to one or another form of illness. In the list of possible symptoms we find many characteristics common enough among ordinary people, including ourselves. When making his diagnosis, the mental therapist seeks to discover if the patient is egotistical, or suspicious, or jealous, or aggressive, or obstinate, or apathetic, and so on. Curiously enough the examination of conscience, given to us as an aid to prepare for confession, bids us ask ourselves: "Am I selfish, or guilty of rash judgment, or jealous, or quarrelsome, or disobedient, or slothful?" To note in ourselves one or more of the tendencies named above, does not, of course, imply that we are destined to become mentally ill. It is only a forecast which indicates that, if we do become mentally ill, our illness will probably be of the type revealed by the analysis.

The foregoing may well serve as warning to you and me that certain habits of ours need much more attention and care than we have been giving them. Moreover, the resemblance of the neurologist's list to the table of sins may remind us that we should bring prayer and sacramental grace to bear on certain disregarded, but dangerous, proclivities of ours.

It is a serious matter if childishness persists for ten, twenty years; if the grown-up man still cannot make up his mind, take a firm resolution, give a definite promise and keep it. Excusably enough, his friends may say to him, "Be your age!" or "Act like an adult!" For an adult should have grown out of habitual fickleness, prolonged hesitation, provoking irresolution, unwillingness to decide. If chronic, and if concerned with serious issues, these symptoms of immaturity may make people reluctant to associate with him; may induce some to suggest gently that they know persons who in similar situations were helped by psychiatry.

Observing the way in which wise guardians train little ones, we note that these children are being taught to resist the promptings of emotion. This is what some of us older persons must learn to do. It is rather humiliating for us if we have to admit that often because we fail to adjust ourselves to the customs prevalent in civilized society, we form an unfavorable contrast to young people, and even to children, who have been intelligently trained. The truth of the matter is that many of us are not even fit to be compared with children trained by stoic Spartans or by imperturbable Indians.

Assuming that we face no unusual problem, we should be

able to educate ourselves to do what the average person does when confronted by obstacles. If brought up in the woods, or on a rough seacoast where nature plays no favorites, where pouting and weeping are of no avail against darkness and winds and tides, people quickly learn to escape from the dominance of some feelings. They "use their heads" — that is, they employ reason and will. The martyrs too, and all the saints, and in fact all faithful Christians, give examples of self-restraint, of moral courage, of fortitude in turning away from pleasure and facing pain.

In the last analysis, the difference between the childish and the mature person seems to lie largely in their comparative ability to appraise the value of an object and the wisdom of an action; and to evaluate the immediate present as against the more or less distant future. The mature person gives higher rating to whatever in the judgment of reasonable men has higher value; and he does first what wise men would agree should first be done. In short, the really mature adjust themselves to that orderly procedure which conforms to reality and is approved by intelligence.

For how long a period must we maintain strict watch over our feelings? Do not the passing years bring balanced judgment? Not always; for emotional pressure on the will is lifelong. True, wide experience and mental growth may combine to make a mature person much more rational than he was in youth. But, on the other hand, persons in middle age, and even beyond that stage, show that they are still subject to emotional pressure, both powerful and unreasonable. If we hear of the "years that bring the philosophic mind," we hear also such phrases as "no fool like an old fool." The phrase "young and foolish" is matched by "old and doting" or "crabbed age"; and we are used to such combinations as "old miser," "old tyrant," "old curmudgeon." King Solomon was acclaimed the wisest of men;

yet showed that age does not always bring more wisdom.

The traditions of Christian civilization demand special respect for the aged; but the aged sometimes forget that this tribute is more a gift than the payment of a strict debt. Think of what the Little Sisters of the Poor have to endure from the old whom they serve! How often is our sympathy aroused by the sight of kindly, gentle persons living with unreasonable aged parents or other relatives!

The physical deterioration which accompanies old age frequently strengthens emotion at the expense of reason, partly because the old are not as pliable as the young, and they tend to resist change, even inevitable change, obstinately. So it is well for us, as we grow old, to avoid assuming that we are better balanced, because we have lived longer; and to keep a restraining hand on our emotions until the very end of our days, so that in the final chapter of life we shall be less unreasonable, less demanding, less conceited than we are inclined to be.

Since conduct in old age will in some degree depend upon a lifelong habit of indulgence, or a lifelong habit of discipline, it is well for those who are still in the formative phase of life to develop now their chances of attaining a kindly, rational, old age. That is the advantage younger persons enjoy — they still have time. It is wise, then, for each of us — not yet atrophied — to make a list of undesirable characteristics commonly associated with old age, in order to see whether or not we are forging them into habits. For at long last, much will depend upon the response we give when God invites us to co-operate with His grace by disciplining ourselves.

It does seem obvious that no really sane man who believes in God would refuse to attempt to discover his own characteristic faults and to train himself to overcome them with the help of grace. Whenever too near the edge of an offense against God, I should stop short and say to myself, "Am I sane?"

ANXIETY

O NE form of anxiety is named "scrupulosity," a word derived from the Latin *scrupulus*, which means a "sharp fragment of stone." If you have ever walked with a pebble in your shoe, you can get a notion of what a scruple may be like. The fact that "scruple" has also been used to denote the smallest unit for measuring time and weight, stresses the idea that a scruple of conscience is in itself an insignificant sort of thing. But spiritual writers tell us that scrupulosity, ridiculously unimportant as it seems to be, may cause serious trouble by inducing fear, indecision, habitual depression. It may be roughly described as an infirmity which prevents an individual from forming a rational judgment as to the moral quality of an act. It makes him uncertain what to do, what to avoid. He sees grave sin where there is no sin at all. He becomes a spiritual cripple. Scrupulosity, therefore, deserves to be discussed at least briefly in these pages. After looking at it objectively, we may be in a position to help ourselves if that should be necessary, or even at times to help others.

To begin with a reassuring general statement: scrupulosity gives no definite clue as to the moral status of the afflicted individual, who may be a grievous sinner or an aspiring saint or a member of that large group of persons who belong to neither class. It falls within the province of both the neurologist and the religious teacher. The neurologist is concerned about the disturbance of the nervous system, whereas the religious teacher is concerned about possible moral fault. In any serious case of scrupulosity, both neurologist and spiritual teacher should work in close co-operation, each taking care not to trespass upon the other's territory. The necessity of this type of co-operation is now generally agreed upon; for, as experts have pointed out, medical science has been drawing closer and closer to the traditional Catholic view, namely, that mind and body are possessed by one and the same individual, and therefore, they affect each other intimately and inevitably.

Spiritual writers discuss scrupulosity extensively. They approach it from various angles, focusing on different aspects, and prescribing the proper course to be taken by a soul afflicted with this painful infirmity, which implies a mental weakness, possibly resulting from emotional disturbance and sometimes associated with a sort of wishful thinking which seeks to substitute something else for the difficult task which true spiritual ambition would impose. At times a scrupulous person, otherwise admirable, is driven into a course of most unreasonable conduct because the exaggerated fear of offending God has so affected his emotions that rational judgment has become impossible.

The Church teaches that sin occurs only when the will freely chooses something known to be under God's prohibition. Before performing an action one should have the approval of conscience, which decides whether the act in question is lawful or unlawful; but, when the mind is incapable of making a rational judgment, conscience is really not functioning. The individual is fearful, confused, panicky, uncertain. In this situation what is one to do? This is the dilemma faced by the scrupulous soul.

A man so well acquainted with the teachings of the Church that he can easily recite the definitions in the catechism, may still, on a particular occasion, be unable to decide whether some particular action is, or is not, a sin. On the one side he sees these considerations; on the other side, those. In a state of mental conflict and unable to decide, he must either go to the altar to receive Holy Communion or stay away. Whichever alternative he chooses, the result is distress, possibly remorse. If the situation described recurs frequently, he may experience a nervous breakdown, or be reduced to a state approaching desperation. Possibly he may abandon the practice of religion because it involves so much pain. Such a person is in obvious need of help. The help may perhaps be obtained from a book of spiritual direction. More probably it will come from a sympathetic confessor who reduces the issue to very simple terms by claiming competence to decide and bidding the penitent disregard his fears as foolish and irrational. The obedience to the confessor will ordinarily suffice to quiet scruples. In the case of a patient who is mentally ill, it may be that he has quite lost his power of willing. If so, he may be in need of treatment by a psychiatrist.

By way of background to the considerations above outlined, it must be kept in mind that scrupulosity is a sort of neurosis — an emotional disturbance which produces an irrational fear, quite out of proportion to the fact. It does not matter how intelligent or how well educated the person in question may be, he may, nevertheless, be totally unable to make an intelligent judgment on the issue now forced upon his attention. If he has enough sense to be humble, to obey, he will thus get back into the world of reality which has been clouded over in his mind. Like a blind person, he must trust and follow a guide. Not to accept advice, not to obey, is to invite the dangers which so often engulf the proud and obstinate, unable to see for themselves and unwilling to accept guidance. Such behavior, quite obviously, has no resemblance to true piety. And that

fact helps us to understand why holy persons, who are sometimes troubled by scruples, are more easily cured because they
endure this trial in the same penitential spirit which leads
them to endure any other kind of suffering.

The moral issue presented by a scrupulous conscience is thus
reduced to a choice between obedience and disobedience. This
is the classical — and notably successful — therapy for scrupulosity. It is based on the sound principle that the confessor is
a better judge than the scrupulous person, and should be
obeyed. Obedience, therefore, involves no risk of offending
God. It is not a surrender of one's conscience. It is the acceptance of medicine prescribed by a spiritual physician. One who
decides to obey — and sticks to his decision, no matter what
fresh emotional disturbances occur — is already on the road to
health. If he continues to do as he is bid, he may well recover;
if he fails to do as he is bid, he may grow worse.

LITTLE THINGS

I N OUR effort to avoid the error of scrupulosity which exaggerates trifles, we must take care not to rush into the opposite extreme by underrating everything which is little. The saint's concern about little things is in sharp contrast with the attitude of the neurotic. The saint does, indeed, take great pains with details; but in this he resembles the gifted artist who combines endless care with genius and thus creates an immortal masterpiece.

The average person comes slowly to a proper appreciation of things apparently insignificant. How long a period passed before prehistoric man realized he could gain control of natural forces by such simple devices as yoking the wind and the stream to mills for the grinding of grain! How recently man became aware that the vapor which issues from boiling water can drive heavy freight trains and luxury liners at breathtaking speed! Scripture gives us many illustrations of the good that results from appreciating what is apparently insignificant — the slingshot of David, the shepherd boy; or the whip of little cords that our Lord used on the money-changers in the Temple; or the still small voice of conscience; or, better yet, the water and oil, the bread and wine, which help the soul to come into intimate sacramental contact with God Himself!

Many a proverb presents in neat phrases the verdict of experience on the value of the insignificant. Sayings which extol the unique worth of little things should strike home to our generation; for we have seen little things rise to an almost incredibly high level of importance. The old yardstick and the foot rule are outmoded by devices too small to be perceived by our unaided senses. The once proud binocular is now a humble relative of the telescope that brings us in touch with sources almost unimaginably distant. Having learned how to employ light, we can now measure a billionth of an inch.

These discoveries remind us of our Lord's warning, not to overlook little things lest we fall "by little and little." We think of little sins which, affecting the soul as fatally as bacteria affect the body, can begin the process that brought King David down to a shameful level. On the other hand, those few words of the penitent thief instantly opened to him the gates of Paradise.

The habit of frequently confessing venial faults may seem to many a minor feature of spiritual life; but it is a promising aid to spiritual progress and a challenge to good will. If we accept that challenge and use confession as the saints used it, we may make our progress in some degree resemble theirs. With this in mind, we may now consider the seemingly minor matter of true sorrow for our habitual venial sins.

To many of us the phrases of the Act of Contrition become overfamiliar by constant repetition. We do, indeed, examine conscience carefully; we do prepare a full and honest account of our — presumably minor — transgressions; we do make a complete recital of our faults. Yet our actual confession may much too closely resemble the type of condescending apology which in social relationships is said to "add insult to injury," for it is not much more than a glib excuse, a polite expression of regret, a mere display of "lip service." If this description applies to our own Act of Contrition, we had better make sure to include in every future confession of even "little faults" some degree of honest sorrow for the past, and some degree of real determination to do better in the future.

In connection with this, we may take encouragement from the fact that very little steps can carry us forward a great distance. One such little step is known as the "Grade A" resolution. This device implies a grim determination to avoid for a brief period one habitual fault which seems comparatively easy to correct. The resolution involves a bargain with oneself to achieve 100 per cent in this project for a short time — perhaps only for a week or even half a week — with a daily check. Note that the length of time is relatively unimportant. The chief point is that the resolution should be a "do-or-die" resolution — unbreakable. The "Grade A" resolution sometimes proves to be so effective that one is surprised at finding the will so much stronger than imagined. All that was needed was intelligent planning. One who takes refuge in the excuse that there is no resolution he can count on himself to carry out for even a minimum period of time, should realize that he is relinquishing the essential dignity of a human person. He is now in need of outside aid.

If one prefers to take a positive rather than a negative resolution, he may choose to do something which will automatically exclude an habitual fault. Thus, for example, if I am in the habit of being two minutes late for Mass, I can focus my resolution on being five minutes early. If I am in the habit of criticizing my neighbor, I can resolve to say something pleasant about him at least once a day. If I often complain of my unhappy lot, I can resolve to give frequent expression to my gratitude for God's gifts to me. This technique is related to the physical principle which bids us to adapt ourselves to the pull of gravity, leaning backward when going down a mountain, and leaning forward when we are going up.

A fact that must ever be kept before us, at least subconsciously, is that we are *always* subject to law. Wishful thinking — which has no force — cannot take the place of willing. Men cannot have a good bridge over a river, or a smooth road through the woods, just by wishing; someone has to plan and construct it. We have received intelligence and will and muscular power for a definite purpose; we must study the physical laws involved in an enterprise and then go to work. Engineers have to determine the strength of a current, the pressure of a tide, the expansion and contraction of a metal, the variations of temperature common in a region. After all that, they must make a plan and labor at it. What is true in the physical order is not less true in the spiritual, although less obvious. Our Lord affirms that the laws governing the spiritual world are definite and irresistible. In their stern insistence on the need of conforming to law, the saints speak even more strongly than the scientists. So do the poets:

> A little more and how much it is,
> A little less, and what miles away.

REHABILITATION

THE Book of Genesis tells us that when God looked at the world He had created, He found it good. Today, its indescribable beauty and magnificence overwhelm us with a sense of His power and His generosity. But then, too, we come upon horrors that have resulted from man's disobedience to God, that mad deed through which, in Milton's words, "came sin into the world and all our woe." Recalling the past history of our race and looking around us at present, we encounter much nauseating wickedness that we can hardly bear to think about. For, if these present years bear witness to man's almost immeasurable power to achieve wonderful results by making use of hitherto latent natural forces, they also oppress us with evidence of dreadful evil that may come through the misuse of those forces. We are now well aware that the exploiting of atomic energy without regard for God's will may even bring about the annihilation of the whole human race.

This provides a good background for reflection on the consequence of sin. As already noted, sin is not only a personal offense, but also a disturbance of the divinely established order, a destruction of something holy. In breaking God's law I set my puny will against the infinite will of the Divine Being upon whom I am totally dependent, to whom I owe my very existence. Even after I have repented and obtained forgiveness, there still remains the violated moral law. God's forgiveness of the insult does not obliterate the injury. It is like a masterpiece defaced and shattered, which can be restored only by some supercosmic force.

The difference between the guilt of a sinner and the effect of his sin becomes clearer when we remember the distinction between what goes on in the mind of a criminal and what happens in the external order — the so-called *corpus delicti* (sometimes mistaken to mean the body of a murdered person). If I try to kill a man whom I hate, but he escapes unhurt, I am, morally speaking, guilty of both an offense against God and a disarrangement of His order. To be forgiven I must first repent; then, after God has pardoned me, I must help to reconstruct what has been destroyed. This reconstruction is far more difficult than what the old alchemists sought to achieve, when they tried to transmute base metal into gold. My soul, twisted into the likeness of the evil one, must again become like God. How can this be done?

We are here upon the threshold of a great mystery — involving the relationship between suffering and sanctity, between love and holiness. One who goes through the New Testament carefully will note the emphasis it places upon this relationship. We know how solicitously our Lord warned His disciples that if they are to follow Him, they must begin by taking up the cross. The Church, carefully treasuring this revelation of the divine value of suffering, stamps it upon the soul of each child of God committed to her care. This is well illustrated in the ceremonies of Baptism when, as the saving water is about to cleanse away original sin, the priest makes the sign of the cross twice on the new Christian saying, "Receive the sign of the cross, both on forehead and on heart and so live that you may be the temple of God." This principle runs counter to our selfish instinct which urges us to evade suffering, even though that suffering is well deserved; but it warns me that I am repudiating my vocation if I try to escape every cross. Nor may I refuse to help others who are unhappy, even though I think they have merited punishment.

By virtue of some dim principle less discernible than the laws which hold the material universe together, spiritual rehabilitation implies an acceptance of suffering by the soul which has defaced its own likeness to God in whose image it was made. When a human being offends God, not only is the moral law broken, but the soul itself is "damaged." We cannot easily find a better comparison than that of a body ravaged by disease. Even when an effective cure is obtained, the recovery is gradual; and during this period of recuperation the physical powers, not yet completely healed, are gradually reconstructed. The soul must come to renewed health and strength, by assimilating God's will more and more perfectly. Eventually, after the soul has made God's will its own, it recovers the original divine likeness bestowed in creation. The degree of recovery, the rate of progress, is measured by the soul's own readiness to suffer whatever, according to God's plan, it should suffer. Rehabilitation is complete when the will actually chooses its own suffering, because that is the will of God.

In purgatory, where the soul is being refashioned in God's image, sinners learn to see and to appropriate the will of God with regard to their own suffering. They perceive the relation between pain and purification. In discussing the difference between the removal of the stain of sin and the payment of the penalty due to sin, St. Thomas Aquinas points out that to a soul, already penitent and pardoned, there is still due a punishment which is to be endured *voluntarily*. "Although satisfactory punishment, absolutely speaking, is against the will, nevertheless, in this particular case and for this particular purpose, it is voluntary." In other words, the soul's contribution to its own rehabilitation takes the form of choosing the punishment. St. Catherine of Genoa describes the souls in purgatory as focusing their attention mainly on God, not on their own pain, which they accept wholeheartedly. Dante pictures a spirit at the very threshold of heaven, not even desiring to be relieved of purgatorial suffering, but longing only for the perfect fulfillment of the will of God. The soul's will is now set on its own pain as once it was set on sin — "*Come fu al peccar, pone al tormento.*"

We may sum it all up in one tremendous statement: "Because my soul, defaced by sin, cannot be restored to Godlikeness except by suffering; and because I shrink from pain; God, who loves me divinely, came down on earth and offered Himself to be crucified. Now He wills my pain; and His will must be my will."

Mankind seems to have an awareness that pain is indeed good medicine. From the days of Job to the present time, great literature has been largely concerned with the sorrows of the just man — a reminder that humanity instinctively relates suffering and sanctity. Too plainly to be ignored, human experience reveals that no high ideal can be faithfully pursued without somehow, somewhere, bringing pain upon someone. "Crossless Christianity" is an absurdity, a monstrosity. Francis Thompson cried out: "Is my pain, after all, the shade of His hand outstretched caressingly?" Coventry Patmore wrote:

> O Pain, Love's mystery,
> Close next of kin
> To joy and heart's delight,
> Low Pleasure's opposite,
> Choice food of sanctity
> And medicine of sin.

REMEMBERING GOD*

IN APPROACHING this subject, we must fit the ideal
of prayer into the whole body of truths taught by
our Lord and formulated by the Church in her official teaching. Sometimes — it may be with the best intentions — we
entertain distorted notions about prayer, perhaps overlooking
the simple fact that prayer is essentially a relationship, an all-
important *inner* relationship, between the soul and God. If a
man is to make progress in prayer, he should be most careful
to wander neither to one extreme nor to the other, not eliminat-
ing God's part or man's. Prayer without God is a meaningless
phrase. Prayer without man is a fantastic offshoot of pantheism.

The only proper attitude for an intelligent creature to take
toward the Infinite Creator is a blending of mind and will in
unreserved adoration. When we are trying to learn how to
pray, we are trying to discover the best way to acquire the
habit of adoring; and whatever helps to establish and maintain
this attitude, helps us to pray. On the other hand, whatever
obstructs adoration, hinders prayer.

Since prayer is a lifting of mind and will to God, and, since
this can be done with or without articulate words, prayer may
be either "vocal" or "mental." This does not imply that prayer
is ever *exclusively vocal*; for the mental element is essential.
But prayer can be *exclusively mental*; for spoken words are
not essential. Words are merely a medium through which the

---

* Reprinted by courtesy of *The Catholic World*.

soul channels to God its hope, its measureless, unending, unutterable longing, its total self-abandonment to His will. The one requisite is that it shall help to put us in touch with God. If we could measure the sincerity of a man who prays, we could probably measure the value of his prayer.

In personal vocal prayers, it does not greatly matter whether we use prose or verse, the Latin language or the vernacular. Nor is a prayer necessarily affected by the age or dignity, the hallowed associations, or the poetic beauty of the words used. It may have originated in the Church's liturgy, or in the writings of the saints; it may be sanctified by the usage of the faithful during centuries, or enriched with many indulgences. The words may be plain or rhymed, polished and eloquent or crudely put together; they may be words made precious by personal association — as, for example, the last words spoken on earth by one we love, and used by us year after year for half a lifetime. The inaudible whisper of a dying man, the half-intelligible lisping of a child, is sometimes more pleasing to God than a petition framed in sonorous words and cultured tone. All this does not mean that no value whatsoever attaches to the words which we read, recite, or compose; but only that they are far less valuable than the disposition of the soul. Better a careful driver with a poor motor, than a poor driver with a powerful motor.

Outsiders sometimes associate the Catholic Church with the practice of "vain repetitions" — a use of mere formulas to which magical effect is attributed. To be sure, there may be Catholics who would do some such thing; but they would be doing it totally in opposition to the Church's teaching. And they surely would not be praying. Prayer, let us recall, is not recitation of a formula, not lip service; it is communion of the soul with God. An illustration of the Church's insistence on the spiritual nature of prayer is the fact that she never imposes a verbal formula upon the Catholic who is communing with God. She does, of course, quite properly, and for obvious reasons, prescribe the exact words to be used in liturgical and sacramental acts; but she does not impose any such obligation on the individual Catholic, or indeed on the priest in his private prayers. Outside of official activities, she never makes any form of words either necessary or sufficient. It is the soul itself which must deal with God; for prayer is communion of spirit with spirit, of creature with Creator.

This attitude of the Church is impressively shown in the way she teaches her children to prepare for that last critical moment of life which will decide their fate in eternity. She ministers to the sick person by means of the Sacraments; she suggests helpful prayers; but she does not teach that the securing of his eternal happiness depends on his uttering of any set of precise words. It depends rather on the soul's inner activities — the man must believe, hope, and love God; he must be sorry for his sins; and, in declaring that these are his sentiments, he may use such words as he feels will best express his attitude of mind and will. It sometimes comes as a surprise to a new convert that the Church trains her children to speak to God thus directly, in their own words, praying simply and sincerely, using formulas only if these are helpful.

The fact that the letter can never take the place of the spirit, that ritual observance can never substitute for faith and love, must not blind us to the value of the liturgy by means of which the Church stimulates and guides the proper approach of the soul to God. The liturgy does, indeed, vary from age to age, and from nation to nation; these variations serve to illustrate its essential unity and Catholicity. We begin to appreciate the high worth of the liturgy when we find that, in urging attendance at the rites of Holy Week, the Church describes them as not only "possessing a unique dignity," but also as containing "special sacramental power for nourishing the Christian life."

Among prayer words which guide and inspire us, we rank first those placed by our Lord on the lips of His disciples. After saying, "Thus shall ye pray," He went on: "Our Father, who art in heaven, hallowed be Thy name, Thy kingdom come, Thy will be done on earth as it is in heaven." Thus He showed us that, when we pray, our thought and will must be turned first to the heavenly Father; and then later we may — and we should — ask for aid for ourselves. Yet we must never seek to impose our own will upon God. Our Lord does promise, "Every request you make in my own name, I myself will grant unto you." Yet to ask "in my own name" obviously means to ask in our Lord's spirit. His spirit was made luminously clear by His prayer in the Garden of Gethsemani: "My Father, if it be possible, let this chalice pass from Me. Nevertheless, not as I will, but as Thou wilt." Only those who pray in this spirit are "asking in His name." Here, perhaps, is one reason why a fervent prayer of ours sometimes remains unanswered.

As to the theme, or tone, of prayer, this may properly vary with the state of the soul. Prayer is "a harp of a thousand strings." One person may be far along the road to holiness; another may be discouraged and almost at the verge of despair.

A vast variety of suggestions with regard to the tone of our prayer is provided in the Gospels and again in the Psalms, particularly those used in the Divine Office. We get help from the *Gloria,* the *Credo,* the various prayers of the Mass, all of which contain words which can be easily shaped into aspirations; and there is always that glorious sequence, *Veni Sancte Spiritus,* which combines poetry and doctrine so inspiringly.

Catholic tradition has been enriched with brief phrases that reflect the close approach of a soul to God. Thus we have our Blessed Mother's *Fiat,* expressing perfect concurrence of a

human will with the divine, and summing up the whole content
of the life of prayer. We remember the cry that came from
the lips of St. Thomas the Apostle, when he looked into the
face of the Master and poured out his soul with "My Lord and
my God!" Then there is that ancient series of aspirations used
by many saints, beginning with *Anima Christi sanctifica me*.
One may repeat just those four words alone countless times;
for they seem to voice the aspirant's hope that his soul will
share something of that uninterrupted contemplation of God
which the soul of Christ possessed.

Spiritual books present us with many aspirations and many
affections. Among such sources is the *Little Book of Eternal
Wisdom* by the Dominican, Blessed Henry Suso. This deserves
particular mention because the author invented his own "Way
of the Cross" by moving from place to place in the chapel after
Matins every night, commemorating at each step a different
scene of our Lord's Passion, and using whatever words he could
find to express pity, gratitude, longing to share the Master's
sufferings. Even today, Suso's method remains a perfectly correct way of "making the Stations" — the devotion without
which our observance of Lent, and particularly of Good Friday, seems incomplete. Much encouragement and also guidance
in the practice of making aspirations comes from Father Augustine Baker, the seventeenth-century Benedictine, whose writings
on contemplative prayer have spread so widely in recent years.
Incidentally, Father Baker held in high esteem *The Spiritual
Exercises* of J. Michael of Coutances, sixteenth-century Carthusian General, whose almost staggering collection of aspirations is probably more elaborate than any other extant.

To assist themselves in praying, many Catholics practice
"meditation" — a procedure that stimulates personal communion
with God by the exercise of memory, understanding, and will.
In this type of mental prayer, a short period is devoted to

reflecting upon whatever subject has been chosen; and the imagination is set at work to form a picture suggestive of devout sentiments. For example, we recall our total dependence upon God, and His goodness as Creator and Redeemer; we dwell upon a scene of our Lord's life that provides a helpful image; we perhaps recall some words of His; and we bring to mind our own selfish tendencies which contrast so sharply with His goodness. Then we speak to God either in words of our own choosing, or by means of a sort of wordless speech that comes from the heart and seems to be composed of resolutions, aspirations, longings rather than of words and sentences. The process of meditation may be undertaken with, or without, the assistance of a book. Sometimes it is varied by what is called "meditative reading," when one follows a text slowly, with interruptions as many and as long as may seem desirable. But whatever procedure is chosen, the aim is always to lift the soul upward and then to speak directly to God.

The practice of organized meditation is inseparably associated with the *Exercises,* prepared by St. Ignatius for use in his training school which, like West Point, has long enjoyed the reputation of forming fine, strong leaders and teachers. Ignatius did not invent the practice of meditation; but he selected, arranged, and pointed out the significance of rules and customs handed down since the days of St. Benedict and even of the Desert Fathers. His method, as explained by Father Roothan, twenty-first General of the Society of Jesus, aims to train beginners so that each man's spiritual development will accord with his particular disposition and enable him to progress toward whatever level of holiness he is destined to occupy. Many a son of St. Ignatius has written books to encourage the progress of souls toward simplicity of prayer.

It is a common experience that, as a result of practicing daily meditation, the share of time given to reasoning tends to become shorter, whereas the share given to aspirations and affections becomes longer. Less varied and more intimate than before, these may be clothed each in a few words, possibly in a single phrase — as when St. Francis passed a whole night saying over and over again, "My God and my All!" The soul's activity will seem like "the fusion of single glances, all directed to the same object," and, like any act repeated frequently, it tends to become habitual. With God thus dominating consciousness, the person who prays may resemble a poet, wordless and motionless, watching "the clouds that gather round the setting sun" or "silent upon a peak in Darien"; or aware of "a Presence closer than breathing." What takes place between the soul and God is like the silent communion of two perfectly sympathetic friends, or — and this is the comparison most often made in spiritual books — the loving attention of a mother to her child. Experts in the science of the spiritual life speak of the "prayer of simplicity or of simple recollection which goes by the name of contemplation, improperly so-called"; and they tell us that by means of it fervent souls may be habitually united to God.

This simpler form of prayer, then, is not something highly complicated, reserved for intellectuals, religious, priests. It is analogous to — if not almost identical with — the attitude of mind and will typical of human beings during their finest hours — the mother, for example, the lover, the poet, the saint. Ordinary persons who can be moved by a symphony orchestra playing Bach or Beethoven under the direction of a master, or who are stirred when the national anthem is sung by a multitude at the moment when their country is on the brink of a national disaster, should be encouraged to undertake affective mental prayer. Christians who are moved by a star-studded sky or a moonlit lake or a perfect flower may well aspire to keep in communion with God, who created these things.

In our efforts to advance in prayer, we do not need to multiply words or mental images. Brother Lawrence, first a soldier, later "a big clumsy footman," finally a lay Brother in the kitchen of a Discalced Carmelite Monastery, tells how, after some years passed in the practice of meditation, he gave up all devotions which were not of obligation in order to devote his efforts to keeping mindful of the presence of God. And, as a sort of watchword, he used the wonderfully luminous adage, "Give all for all." In a precious and widely read small volume, the Jesuit Father Caussade's *Abandonment to Divine Providence,* we find the kernel of his teaching in a matchless phrase, "The sacrament of the present moment." This conveys the idea that at each moment of our lives we are in contact with a sort of sacramental envelope containing a hidden grace, ready to be received by anyone who has the right dispositions.

Then there is always that unique little handbook of holiness, *The Imitation of Christ,* which reflects the teachings of the Gospel so impressively that it has kept spreading far and wide for almost six hundred years. As George Eliot said, the medieval "monk" who wrote it represented a countless number of men "who, ages ago, felt, and suffered, and renounced, in the cloister perhaps, with serge gown and tonsured head, with much chanting and long fasts, and with a fashion of speech different from ours, but under the same silent, far-off heavens, and with the same passionate desires, the same failures, the same weariness." That small volume (whether from Thomas à Kempis or Gerard Groote) is still saying to each one of us: "If thy heart were right then every creature would be to thee a mirror of life and a book of holy doctrine."

A habit of "awareness," a sense of God's presence, may come as a result of diligent effort on the part of the individual soul, aided by what is called *ordinary* grace. This is quite in line with all growth, which results from a conforming to divine laws.

But if progress in prayer is truly something quite normal, then we face this problem: "Do the majority of persons capable of acquiring habitual awareness of God's presence, actually acquire it; and, if not, why not?"

A partial explanation may be found in our common human tendency to overdo things, to use too many words, ideas, images; or in that other tendency to become timid and distrustful whenever there is question of spiritual progress. But, instead of indulging in private speculation about the answer to the question, it seems wise to listen to a great saint, made Doctor of the Church because of his unique competence in the field of prayer — St. John of the Cross. In more than one passage he imparts the rather startling information that he believes the gift of contemplation may be hoped for by all baptized Christians. Facing the problem created by the large percentage who never actually attain to contemplative prayer, he explains that this happens because God finds only a few who permit Him to work His will in them. "There are many who, when He sends them trials, instead of submitting with perfect patience, refuse to endure dryness and mortification." In other words, a multitude who would be able to make progress in prayer are not willing to pay the price.

St. John seems to be re-echoing *The Imitation of Christ*: "No one is fit to comprehend heavenly things who has not resigned himself to suffer adversities for Christ." So here, as always, the cross is still the symbol of our religion. Self-denial opens our eyes and steels our wills; and grace propels us along the way followed by Brother Lawrence: "I worshiped Him the oftenest I could, keeping my mind in His Presence, and recalling it as often as I found it wandering from Him."

DEATH

Newman's epitaph, chosen by the great Cardinal himself, shows what he had in mind when he used the words: *Ex umbris et imaginibus in veritatem.* He was moved by the same idea which imposes itself on you and me and every Christian when we think of death — that the present life is shadow not substance; image not reality. After death — but only then — we shall be united to God, to Infinite Truth, Goodness, Beauty, Love. This notion of the relation between life and death is an essential part of the Faith, revealed by Christ, preserved by the Church, communicated to each one of us when we are instructed in our religion. To be sure, not everyone of us lives up to its implications; yet we are truly Christian only in the measure that we do. And indeed, it seems quite safe to say that we are not even rational, except in the measure that we adjust our lives to the Christian notion of death.

One point that deserves particular attention is the contrast between our certainty that death will come and our uncertainty as to the time of its coming. Thomas à Kempis, who reads souls so accurately and prescribes for human needs so skillfully, emphasizes this over and over again. To persons familiar with his homely lessons there comes to mind every so often something like an echo of his words: "Remember that time once lost never returns." "Those who do not shun small defects will by

little and little fall into greater." "Watch over thyself; stir
up thyself; and whatever cometh to others, neglect not thyself."
"Live as though thou wert immediately to die." "Better fly sin
than be afraid of death." "If unprepared today, how dost thou
know that thou wilt be alive tomorrow?"

We must face the stern fact that death is the implacable
foe of all animal life, on both the human and the lower level.
Each individual being is stirred at the approach of this imper-
sonal, soulless force whose irresistible pressure brings physical
annihilation. Each individual reacts to its approach with an
instinctive struggle, foredoomed to failure. By social conven-
tion, by a sort of "gentlemen's agreement," these frightening
facts are commonly excluded from ordinary conversation —
although they are of infinitely greater moment to each individual than the gravest issues concerning wealth, rank, prestige,
popularity, physical comfort. It is because we do not ordinarily
give these unpleasant subjects the attention they deserve that
they are thrust upon the reader at the present moment.

Only by imagining the circumstances in which we shall come
to the end of life, can we get what may be called a "working
notion" of unknown factors. We find ourselves unable — and
perhaps more than half unwilling — to foretell when and where
and how life will come to a close. On the one hand, this in-
ability gives me a sort of illusory comfort; but, on the other
hand, it presents me with countless specific problems — questions of enormous importance, questions that I am totally
unable to answer, questions that involve my prospects of everlasting joy or sorrow. It is folly not to prepare carefully for
any grave situation into which I shall be thrust eventually; and,
if it is a matter of my death, I cannot possibly afford to be
unready. The insurance agent reminds me that I must foresee
certain possibilities and some probabilities; but none of these is
so sure and so significant as the certainty that one day I must

face God. What if on that dread day I should not be ready?
A preacher sometimes bases his sermon on the text, "It is
appointed unto men once to die, and, after this, the judgment." Not only on the occasion of a sermon, but also at other
times, and indeed very frequently, this text deserves to be
studied. What gives death its great significance is, of course,
the judgment — the judgment which will propel the soul into
another life that will never end, whether for weal or for woe.
The twenty-fifth chapter of St. Matthew's Gospel records the
words in which our Lord presented an unforgettable picture,
separating His enemies from His friends, sinners from saints,
those destined for unending misery from those destined for
eternal happiness. It is not easy to bring ourselves to the
realization that all this is true; yet, not to believe it, is to
reject Christ's teaching. Even more difficult is it for us to
realize that the coming of death is incomparably more certain
than the dawning of tomorrow's sun. We may shrink from
facing this truth with open eyes. Yet here it is; and there is no
Christian way, there is not even any sane way, of ignoring it
or of minimizing its significance. Little wonder that the man
who keeps the thought of death before him, the man who
looks at life through God's eyes, the man who beholds the
present and the future not in the light of his own petty interests, but in the light of eternity, he, and only he, is said to see
things as they really are.

EPILOGUE: VISION OR NIGHTMARE

(The lines below by an old priest seem to offer themselves as a fitting epilogue to this volume.)

I SHALL never forget that night. As for the preceding day I recall only that to a wavering Catholic, I had spoken about St. Teresa's vision of her own possible place in hell and, while instructing a prospective convert, I had dwelt upon the omnipresence of God. In the evening I had made my too nearly perfunctory weekly confession, skipped through five decades of the Rosary and gone to bed. I was soon asleep, and then suddenly I was awake — just that — awake, and no more. It was impossible to know if my soul was in my body, for I could feel nothing — not hands or feet or lips or tongue. "Am I completely paralyzed?" I asked myself. "Have I been buried alive?" "Am I enclosed in a casket or shut in by stones or victim of an accident?" I could not say, nor could I remember having been anointed or hearing the prayers for the dying. Perhaps that perfunctory earlier confession had really been my last.

Repeatedly I asked myself, "Is this purgatory? Is it hell?" "Is this what St. Teresa experienced?" Using my one active faculty, I recalled the many ways in which I had acted like the ultramoderns — the self-reliant people who leave God quite out of their calculations. "Is that the cause of my present condition?" I asked myself: "Has He taken me at my word, and left me utterly to my own resources? Has He let me go into eternity on my own? If so, I am indeed in hell."

Then, like a sudden light dispelling abysmal darkness, came the thought: "God is here: He must be here. There is no place where God is not. What are you looking at, thinking of, wondering about? Look at Him! Give Him all you have to give of attention, and thought, and desire and will! Adore Him!" And this I tried to do. Then I said, "Do not leave me, Lord!" And I did not exactly *hear*, but rather seemed *to be aware* of our Lord answering me: "No, I will not leave you; but be careful that you do not leave me." So I changed my prayer. Instead of "Do not leave me, dear Lord," I kept saying, "I will not leave You, dear Lord," using as a sort of refrain the words of St. Thomas, "My Lord, and my God," and of St. Francis, "My God and my All!"

I have never forgotten that experience. I have the habit of recalling it, whenever I am tempted or depressed or sorry for myself or beginning to get absorbed in petty affairs. I frequently get straightened out by saying to myself: "What are you looking at, thinking of, planning for? Dear Lord, forgive! You are here! You I honor, worship, adore! Your will, Your will, Your holy will, be done!"

That ends my story. The telling of it may well be of help to you. Crowded as our minds are with plans and hopes and joys and fears and failures, we must stop now and then to ask ourselves: "Am I more concerned with other aims than that of pleasing God?" If so, we are like sheep on the edge of a precipice. We must say to ourselves: "Wake up! Wake up! God is here."